EVA GORE-BOOTH
AND
ESTHER ROPER

a biography

Gifford Lewis is the author of *Somerville & Ross: The World of the Irish R.M.*; Her *Selected Letters of Somerville & Ross* will be published by Faber in Spring 1989. Born in Edinburgh in 1945, and brought up in Wales, she had art college training in lettering and graphics, and worked in publishing in Ireland from 1968. She was designer at the Irish University Press until 1972, when she founded, with Clare Craven, the firm of Gifford & Craven, publishing mainly art history and special editions. She now lives in Oxford.

This book is dedicated to
ALBERT OWEN RANKIN
first cousin to my father,
who was interned from 1915–1919
in Penderyn CO Camp, Dartmoor Prison,
Pentonville Prison, Wakefield Prison,
and Wormwood Scrubs.

Eva
GORE BOOTH
— AND —
Esther
ROPER

A BIOGRAPHY

GIFFORD LEWIS

PANDORA

London   Sydney   Wellington

First published by Pandora Press, an imprint of the Trade Division of
Unwin Hyman, in 1988.

PANDORA PRESS

Unwin Hyman Limited
15/17 Broadwick Street
London W1V 1FP

Unwin Hyman Inc
8 Winchester Place, Winchester, MA 01890

Allen & Unwin Australia Pty Ltd
PO Box 764, 8 Napier Street, North Sydney, NSW 2060

Allen & Unwin NZ Ltd (in association with the Port Nicholson Press)
60 Cambridge Terrace, Wellington, New Zealand

British Library Cataloguing in Publication Data

Lewis, Gifford, *1945*–
   Eva Gore-Booth and Esther Roper.
   1. Great Britain. Women's suffrage
   movements. Gore-Booth, Eva, & Roper,
   Esther, 1870–1926
   I. Title
   324.6′23′0922

   ISBN 0–86358–159–5

Set in 10 on 11 point Sabon by
Computape (Pickering) Ltd, Pickering, North Yorkshire
and printed in Great Britain by Cox & Wyman Ltd, Reading

CONTENTS

ILLUSTRATIONS

GLOSSARY

ILP	Independent Labour Party 1893
L & CWT & OWRC	Lancashire and Cheshire Women Textile and Other Workers Representation Committee 1903
MNSWS	Manchester National Society for Women's Suffrage 1867–97
NCF	No-Conscription Fellowship 1915
NESWS	North of England Society for Women's Suffrage 1897
NUWSS	National Union of Women's Suffrage Societies 1897
NUWT	National Union of Women Teachers 1919
WEA	Workers' Educational Association 1903
WILPF	Women's International League for Peace and Freedom 1915
WSPU	Women's Social and Political Union 1903
WTLC	Women's Trades and Labour Council, Manchester 1904
WTUC	Women's Trades Union Council, Manchester 1895–1919

ACKNOWLEDGEMENTS

I wish to thank the following: Miss J. M. Ayton, Archivist, Manchester Central Library; Margaret Bonfiglioli; Philippa Brewster; Mrs B. Bryan of Deganwy; Thomas Charles-Edwards; Clare Craven, Gifford & Craven, Dublin; David Doughan at the Fawcett Library; Miss Aideen Gore-Booth, Lissadell; Josslyn and Jane Gore-Booth; Josephine de Goris; Isobel Harvey; Marij van Helmond, The Pankhurst Trust, Manchester; Catherine Ireland at the Fawcett Library; Rosemary Keen, Archivist, Church Missionary Society; Mrs G. M. leggatt of Stockport; Jill Liddington; Charles W. Mann of the Pattee Library, Pennsylvania State University; Gemma O'Connor; Miss C. L. Penney, C.M.S. Archives, Birmingham University; Lana Pringle; P. R. Quarrie, Librarian, Eton College; Dr Hilary Robinson; Jeanne Sheehy; F. B. Singleton, Librarian, *The Guardian*, Manchester; Serena Surman in the Modern Papers Reading Room, Bodleian Library, Oxford; David Taylor, Local History Librarian, Central Library, Manchester; Michael Wynne, National Gallery of Ireland.

Particular thanks are due to Josslyn and Jane Gore-Booth for kindly allowing me to work on Eva Gore-Booth's papers at their home; to David Taylor for his knowledge and intuitive skills in using his local history archive at Manchester – it was he who identified the Rev. Edward Roper – but without Jill Liddington's work I would not have known which questions to ask and thus prompt this discovery. Special thanks also to Margaret Bonfiglioli for research assistantship in Manchester Women's Suffrage Papers and the Fawcett Library, and for driving me from Oxford to Lissadell to arrive on time.

The photographs of the Round House, Lissadell, Frognal Gardens and the grave of Eva Gore-Booth and Esther Roper are by the author. Other illustrations are from the collection of Josslyn Gore-Booth, apart from the 1906 Women's Suffrage deputation to Campbell-Bannerman, by kind permission of Nelson Public Library; 83 Heald Place, The Round House Plan, and Jersey Buildings are by kind permission of Manchester Public Library. The photograph of the memorial window to E. G.-B. is reproduced by kind permission of the Historical Collections, Labor Archive, Pattee Library, Pennsylvania State University.

Mrs G. M. Leggatt and Mrs B. Bryan were both pupils of Constance Andrews who wrote to me in response to a request for information in the *Manchester Evening News*. Thanks are due to them both for allowing me to quote from their accounts of the Church of the New Age.

I have to thank Michael Yeats for allowing me to quote from 'In memory of Eva Gore-Booth and Con Markievicz' and from some letters of W. B. Yeats, and Virago for allowing me to quote Sylvia Pankhurst's description of Eva Gore-Booth. Quotations from the Women's Suffrage Papers in Manchester are by permission of Manchester Central Library. Quotations from the papers of Teresa Billington Greig are by kind permission of the Fawcett Library, as are the quotations from the short-lived journal *The Barmaid*, which was brought to my attention by Catherine Ireland, and the longer-surviving journal *Urania*, brought to my attention by David Doughan.

INTRODUCTION

Consumption was once a deadly disease beyond the doctor's skills to control. It pervaded all ranks of society. The richer classes, by travel and costly sanatorium treatment, could delay death, but not avoid it. The grim weather of the British Isles made them a perfect breeding ground for the pulmonary diseases that were associated with consumption and many a pale and listless young Britisher with a hacking cough went 'abroad' in search of health on doctor's orders. Happily, not all of them turned out to be consumptives, and Eva Gore-Booth and Esther Roper who met in Italy in 1896, by chance, as such a pair of invalids were two such cases of reprieve.

Up to the time of their meeting neither of them seemed to have been very happy. Esther Roper was twenty-eight, her father had died when she was eight and her mother when she was twenty. She was bringing up her brother Reginald, eight years younger than herself. She had been at the deathbeds of both her father and his brother in the same week in 1877 (both died of pulmonary diseases) and Esther was sent to Italy with 'a weak chest' and exhaustion brought on by overwork. She was not a woman of independent means – she earned her living as a suffrage union organiser working in the factories and slums of industrial Manchester.

She was a dedicated worker and drove herself unceasingly without holidays. When she became ill her professors and tutors at Owens College, who were Italophiles and frequently visited expatriate British in Italy, sent her to Italy with an introduction to George MacDonald, the novelist, who had also left Manchester for Italy because of suspected consumption.

Esther was a house guest at the MacDonald villa at Bordighera when, one day, standing under an olive tree in the garden, a batch of fresh guests arrived. A Miss Gore-Booth, an Anglo-Irish gentlewoman, tall, short-sighted and vague-looking, was introduced to Miss Roper, the women's suffrage organiser from Manchester. Eva Gore-Booth was introspective and not, at this stage, noted for talking. We can only speculate as to what instantly made for communication between these two women. Eva had known that income came to the family from estates at Salford by Manchester, she had an interest in the 'woman question', and she had probably not met the combination of woman graduate and suffrage organiser before. She was overcome by curiosity. Esther recalled many years later:

> At once I was met by an impetuous stream of questions. What work were we doing for the working women? What was going on in the franchise movement? How did people work and live in an industrial centre in Manchester?

This was no idle conversation-making, these two voices were to carry on sounding each other out for the next thirty years. Esther describes their decision to live together in her introduction to *The Complete Poems of Eva Gore-Booth*, published in 1929. As we can see, Esther had a genius for self-effacement and contraction. She writes briskly:

> We spent the days walking and talking on the hillside by the sea. Each was attracted to the work and thoughts of the other, and we became friends and companions for life – she made up her mind to join me in the work in Manchester.

They remained perfectly calm, certain and unselfconscious about their love for each other for the rest of their lives. They were fortunate in living at a time when ladies could still set up home together and live in perfect equanimity with no suspicion of the dark wastes of psychopathology into which they had strayed. They remain a shining example of what might be achieved by the pairing of women who refuse to have their lives ruled by their reproductive systems, and if they did not have children they certainly had peace and love. Eva was more expansive about their meeting than Esther, in a poem she wrote:

Was it not strange that by the tideless sea
the jar and hurry of our lives should cease,
That under olive boughs we found our Peace
And all the world's great song in Italy?

In their time Esther Roper and Eva Gore-Booth were seen as a pair of oddities who did not fit into any tidy categorisation within the official women's suffrage movement and have inevitably 'disappeared from history' along with many other women. When we find brief accounts of Roper and Gore-Booth there is little to tell us exactly why this pair is not 'of proud memory' to the women's movement. The average brief biographical note, for example, tells us that Eva Gore-Booth brought to the suffrage movement something of the burning sense of injustice which was entirely new in the humdrum round of British suffrage societies; That many of E.G.-B.'s campaigns were unconventional. While in Manchester she formed the Manchester Barmaids' Association, in this she was helped by Miss Roper. That other campaigns included; work on behalf of women gymnasts, circus performers and the flower-sellers of Oxford Circus.

Definitely, they were unconventional, but just as definitely they were retiring, withdrawn and lived an intensely private life. Jill Liddington, who attempted to uncover Roper's early life for *One Hand Tied Behind Us*, wrote:

Esther Roper was an extremely reticent woman with a marked distaste for personal exposure. She remains almost anonymous behind the organisations through which she worked and seems to have preferred the role of *eminence grise* to that of platform personality.

Roper and Gore-Booth broke with the Pankhursts; having been the mentors of the young Christabel they were horrified by her adoption of violence, and always (rather loosely) remained attached to the conservative and 'staid' National Union of Women's Suffrage Societies (NUWSS) led by Mrs Fawcett. Within this wing of the movement the pair were certainly freakish and it is not difficult to understand why their apparently eccentric close and lifelong involvement with working-class women and their extremely unorthodox public views on sexuality should have combined in the mind of an average NUWSS suffragist to give the pair an aura of 'not quite respectable'. It may be that their lack of repute arises from the fact that the pair were in some way 'unmentionable' and were not talked about.

Some evidence to support this came to light in the late 1970s. Susan Gubernat, an American scholar, approached the Gore-Booth family for assistance with a life of Eva, and Lady Gore-Booth thought to trace old suffragists who had worked with Eva:

> Lady Clare Annesly, Lady Constance Mallinson, Mrs Hazel Hunkins-Hallinan, and Dame Margery Corbett-Ashby. The first would have been 87, the second 95 and the third 84, if indeed they were still alive. But I did manage to speak to Dame Margery, who was 96 or 97 at the time (she has since died) and she spoke of Eva and Esther as follows:
>
> 'I remember EG-B as one of a pair of brilliant friends. I cannot remember the other one's name. They acted as a tonic and challenge to the suffrage movement and Liberal head-quarters. Their ideas were not always orthodox but we wel-comed their visits. I admired EG-B and enjoyed working with her.'

Where Eva's memory survives she tends to be described as a minor poetess and sister of the more famous Countess Markie-vicz; her lifelong partnership and work with Esther Roper is rarely mentioned, if at all. As Dame Margery's recollection shows us, even fellow suffragists did not care to remember Esther Roper's name; they did not put a name to that aspect of suffragism that provided so much of its driving force – the pairing of women. There were many such as Eva and Esther, like Eleanor Rathbone and Elizabeth Macadam, whose talents and energies were phenomenal but who have not been given recognition because of their 'unorthodoxy'.

Present-day notions of sexual freedom have allowed expansion of 'free' love between men and women, but as pairing relation-ships have come to be seen as primarily sexual such pairings as Eva's and Esther's are now seen as unnatural; yet during the days of the women's suffrage movement such pairings were frequent, looked upon as natural and were evidently beneficial. Most prob-ably the point of departure for Eva and Esther into unorthodoxy in the public eye was with the foundation and publication of the journal *Urania* in 1916, discussed in Chapter 9. Although this was printed for private circulation its ideas reached a wide circle, or at least rumours of its ideas spread to give it a certain reputation. *Urania*'s reputation must have been wildly eccentric when we realise that it asked its readers to give up masculinity and femininity at a time when the most emancipated female trend-setters were learning to take rapturous pleasure in insemination and its consequences.

By using *Urania* as the name of their journal they chose what would appear now to be a controversial title, the name having suffered the same change of meaning as 'gay'. It has become associated with homosexuality. For example, we find Germaine Greer in her *Sex and Destiny* referring to the 'Uranian lifestyle' of Edward Carpenter. But in Eva and Esther's time the word had a perfectly respectable classical past and we need look no further than Milton, who was read thoroughly by any young ladies with a competent governess or teacher, to understand the nature of the Urania invoked by Eva and Esther.

Milton addresses Urania at the opening of Book VII of *Paradise Lost* as the Muse of heaven:

> Descend from heav'n, Urania, by that name
> If rightly thou art called, whose voice divine
> Following, above th' Olympian hill I soar,
> Above the flight of Pegasian wing.

Pegasus was the winged steed of the Muses, used to symbolise flights of the imagination. Eva used the winged horse also as a graphic symbol in her drawings. The Muse Urania was the patroness of astronomy, an all-important subject to those theosophists and mystics like Eva who studied astrology.

Some form of panic must have set in about the meaning of Urania even in the second decade of this century as the Common Rooms of women's colleges in Oxford refused to take *gratis* copies, but the Common Rooms may well have panicked over *Urania*'s content. Although the journal does have an interest in accidental changes of sex (muscular peasant girl leaps over wall and finds male genitals have descended, etcetera) that is at first disconcerting, the main line of the journal is towards a sexual equalising by a reduction of learnt, theatrical differences between the sexes. *Urania* was not preaching homosexuality as an escape from child-bearing. A review claimed: 'the "manly man" and the "womanly woman" are just as ugly and imperfect as the effeminate youth and the masculine maiden' and in aiming at a sexual perfection *Urania* did not want to praise perversion, but it certainly preached a kind of mental hermaphroditism.

It quoted a French curé who advised the children in his village 'Let the boys be tender: let the girls be strong', and when amazed parents remonstrated that surely he had muddled up his advice he replied: No, for Nature has already done its worst in that direction. Fashions of thought as to what is 'natural' and 'Nature' change. Eva and Esther lived at a time and in a small section of society when they were able to believe that changes could be made in the nature of women and men, and they believed in the intense mental effort of nurturing this change: that men could unlearn aggression as the leading edge of character, that women could unlearn submissiveness and silence in the face of this aggression. As society has become increasingly genitalised their efforts may seem now futile and eccentric but their message to women is still intelligible: to be human is to be more than animal.

They refused to accept sex as a foundation stone in life and they did seem to feel disdain and pity for those whose lives – as a *Urania* review snapped – 'were ruled by their pelvic regions'. They were disturbed by the animalism of men's image of women, but more disturbed by the women who incarnated it. They put aside sexuality from their lives as an irrelevance, Eva calmly noting in a manuscript book of dream images that she had not bothered to record any that were 'obviously sexual'. It is difficult to discover the tone of their private life together. No papers survive, as their decision to work and live together was taken so quickly that there are no letters between them. There are a few notebooks in the possession of the Gore-Booth family and little miscellaneous ephemera.

They were not possessive of each other. Esther searched out specialists in subjects that interested Eva, and found her new friends, even in the last months of her life. They had an enormous circle of friends – their men friends tending to be from the Men's League for Women's Suffrage and from the ranks of conscientious objectors. They gave their time prodigally to causes, and personal cases of difficulty. In a sense they gave themselves away, utterly. They are almost depersonalised by their degree of compassion.

We find pairing between women both early and late in the

women's suffrage movement from Frances Power Cobbe and Mary Lloyd to Eleanor Rathbone and Elizabeth Macadam but a remarkable pair contemporary with Eva Gore-Booth and Esther Roper was Catherine Middleton and Margaret MacDonald. Theirs was an undisguised cross-class pairing – Middleton was working class – whereas Roper and Gore-Booth have always been taken for a pair of gentlewomen. These two pairs came into conflict over the employment of barmaids issue but nevertheless typify the union between equals and women. It was easier for women to work in pairs and as more and more educated women took to professions we find them chiefly in the fields of education, journalism, social work and politics.

Women graduates paired to found girls' schools, like Eva and Esther's friends Miss Neild and Miss Gill with their school, Pinehurst, in Surrey, undeterred by echoes of Miss Buss and Miss Beale, and Margaret Kemp, one of the most gifted of Esther's fellow students at Owens, opened a school with her sister. There were prolific writing partnerships between women, and Edith Somerville and Martin Ross joined Eva and Esther's Industrial and Professional Women's Suffrage Society (The Ind. and Prof.). Others were Katherine Bradley and Edith Cooper, writing together as Michael Field, the sisters Emily and Dorothea Gerard writing together as E. D. Gerard, and the fascinating missionary pair Mildred Cable and Francesca French wrote travel books together.

In politics working partnerships operating in the same areas as Eva and Esther were Cicely Hamilton and Bessie Hatton with the Women Writers Suffrage League (an auxiliary of the NUWSS), Ada Nield Chew with Mary Macarthur in the Women's Trade Union League, and Christabel Pankhurst with Annie Kenney in the Women's Social and Political Union (WSPU). Friendships were very important to highly articulate women who were learning the art of public-speaking and just one example of a pair exhilarated by each other – though any bystanders must have been exhausted and deafened – was Selina Cooper and Harriette Beanland. During their time in Manchester, Eva and Esther did not commonly operate together, Eva working with Sarah Dickenson and Esther with Sarah Reddish in different organisations.

Few prophet and disciple relationships between women turned as sour as the relationship between Eva Gore-Booth and Christabel Pankhurst – New Women were actually proud to be formed in their youth by love and admiration for an older woman in the suffrage movement. Helena Swanwick's frank acknowledgement of the mentorship of Rachel Scott, wife of C. P. Scott, is very moving, and shows that such influence is life-long and a female construction of the common male-bonding between teacher and pupil. In Manchester in the 1890s teachers like Alice Crompton and the wonderful Miss Winstanley – who sadly for Manchester transferred to University College Aberystwyth – had a vital influence on their pupils' lives.

Female acolytes have given us the best biographies of suffragists, like the outstanding life of Mrs Fawcett by Ray Strachey. There are sadly few of such published biographies but as caches like the Billington Greig Papers are edited and published, and as more personality and humanity enlarges our knowledge of the women in the women's suffrage movement, so we may avoid their dreadful reduction to 'sample women' in computerised surveys of the abnormal in social history.

It would be wrong to assume that all pairs of women were lesbian; when they were they took very little trouble to conceal it, like Katherine Bradley and Edith Cooper, ecstatically ignorant of Freud. Strong-minded women who loved each other had a quite remarkable unself-consciousness about physical desire. Ethel Smyth is a most helpful source here. Women, married and single, who might incline to physical affairs with other women actually did so if the opportunity presented itself; others didn't incline, and although women might form pairs this does not infallibly indicate a desire for lesbian love. Edith Somerville, so innocent as to come to the pass of sleeping in a double bed with Ethel Smyth on a holiday in Italy, responded negatively to an attempted seduction: 'My amazement! My Surprise!' and Smyth's passion withered in Somerville's laughter. Some female pairings were quite formal: like Ivy Compton-Burnett and Margaret Jourdain, Eva Gore-Booth and Esther Roper never entered each other's bedrooms except in illness.

Reginald Roper, like his sister, covered his tracks very thoroughly and it is possible that the enormous difficulty of discovering anything about the Roper family was due to Reginald and Esther's reluctance to reveal their working-class origins as they both acquired and developed the tastes and manners of the upper-middle classes. A persistent rumour that Reginald Roper taught at Eton cannot be substantiated by any records. In his sister's will he is described rather grandly as 'educational consultant' – this may be a euphemism for a supply-teacher.

In looking at the suffrage movement from the viewpoint of Esther Roper and Eva Gore-Booth we cannot fail to be depressed by the personalities of Emmeline and Christabel Pankhurst. Great women they may have been in some aspects but it is painful to admit that to the jaundiced eye they could seem opportunistic charmers who instantly dropped people no longer of any use to them. Incontrovertible facts, for example relating to Emmeline Pankhurst's treatment of her daughter Sylvia and her son Harry, or Christabel's treatment of the Pethick-Lawrences, that are appalling in themselves, have been enlarged upon in *Queen Christabel*, a grossly chauvinist study by David Mitchell that is rightly abhorred by feminists; but the facts remain, and as more memoirs like those of Teresa Billington Greig and Helena Swanwick become available the mists of Pankhurst worship will, hopefully, disperse and the great and intelligent efforts of their contemporaries come to be valued and celebrated.

CHAPTER 1

THE CHILDHOOD OF EVA GORE-BOOTH

The sisters Constance and Eva Gore-Booth belong to a remarkable group of Anglo-Irish rebels against the status quo, like Parnell, Mrs Despard, Maud Gonne and Casement, whose close relationships with powerful English institutions and families helped to bring about the dismantling of English government of Ireland from within.

The ancestors of the Gore-Booth family settled in Ireland in Elizabethan times; their estates covered 25,000 acres of County Sligo. Towards the end of the nineteenth century the children of Sir Henry Gore-Booth, the Arctic explorer, broke the bands of landlord orthodoxy that had satisfied the family for so many generations. Among Sir Henry's five children were Constance, born in 1868, who became Countess Markievicz, 'The Rebel Countess' and one of the leaders of the 1916 rebellion; Josslyn, born in 1869, who introduced co-operative practices to Sligo and became the first landlord in Ireland to sell his estate to his tenants after the 1903 Land Act as an act of principle; and Eva, born in 1870, the poetess and suffragist who worked for years amongst the poor of Manchester.

The Gore-Booth home, Lissadell, is in the heart of what is now called 'Yeats country' and in the winter of 1894–5 Yeats was twice a guest at this hospitable house. He underestimated the Gore-Booth capacity for action; to him Sir Henry 'thinks of nothing but the north pole' and Josslyn, his heir, got this notice:

The eldest son is 'theoretically' a home ruler and practically some kind of humanitarian, much troubled by his wealth and almost painfully conscientious . . . . He is not however particularly clever and has not, I imagine, much will . . .

He thought the girls beautiful and graceful, and encouraged Eva, to whom he was strongly attached, to persevere with her poetry. He did not expect either girl to take any active part in life. In 1916 he wrote to Eva to comfort her when Constance was apparently under sentence of death: 'your sister and yourself, two beautiful figures among the great trees of Lissadell, are among the dear memories of my youth'. Later Yeats refined this memory into a poem 'In memory of Eva Gore-Booth and Constance Markievicz', dated October 1927.

> The light of evening, Lissadell,
> Great windows open to the south,
> Two girls in silk kimonos, both
> Beautiful, one a gazelle.
> But a raving autumn shears
> Blossom from the summer's wreath;
> The older is condemned to death,
> Pardoned, drags out lonely years
> Conspiring among the ignorant.
> I know not what the younger dreams –
> Some vague Utopia – and she seems,
> When withered old and skeleton-gaunt,
> An image of such politics.
> Many a time I think to seek
> One or the other out and speak
> Of that old Georgian mansion, mix
> Pictures of the mind, recall
> That table and the talk of youth,
> Two girls in silk kimonos, both
> Beautiful, one a gazelle.
> Dear shadows, now you know it all,
> All the folly of a fight
> With the common wrong or right
> The innocent and the beautiful
> Have no enemy but time
> Arise and bid me strike a match
> And strike another till time catch;

> Should the conflagration climb,
> Run till the sages know.
> We the great gazebo built,
> They convicted us of guilt;
> Bid me strike a match and blow.

The poem reveals Yeats' sadness, almost disgust, at the careers of Eva and Constance as political activists; to him they now seem shrill and wasted and to have lost their beauty. In common with other writers of the Celtic Revival, Yeats had a totemic vision of women as little more than beautiful icons, inspirational but not themselves inspired. Two pleasing and pretty girls inexplicably to Yeats threw away all the advantages of their privileged birth. Neither Constance nor Eva was tempted to play the traditional feminine role available to them; children and domesticity did not present a complete and satisfying world in itself; they wanted, and got, a great deal more from life than was at the time allowed for their sex and their class.

English high society laid great store by descent from the Norman, or one of his supporters, who became 'Conqueror' of England in 1066. By another adroit Norman conquest, and at the invitation of Dermot MacMurrough, king of Leinster, England came to govern Ireland – the top layer of society in Ireland came to have set English ways, and after 1800 the centre of government, and high society, was London.

In the mid-nineteenth century, with the intense involvement and application of scholars and archaeologists in what has been called 'the rediscovery of Ireland's past' there came a slow-creeping awareness in some alert sections of the class called Anglo-Irish that their natural 'overlordship' of a country with a language as ancient and as complex as Sanskrit, with laws, customs and legends of such antiquity, and manuscripts of such remarkable beauty, was indeed questionable.

The English language is a newcomer in the history of language, an offshoot of Germanic, and is set in its modern form only in Chaucer's time. Irish branched off from the main Indo-European stock a full thousand years before Anglo-Saxon branched off from Germanic. In medieval Ireland native speakers were horrified by the English language which they thought barbarous, 'clattering' and ugly. The study of ancient Irish laws, poetry and legends proceeded apace in the late nineteenth century, the Gaelic

League was founded in 1893, and the language and literature of Ireland soon became a powerful propaganda tool in the struggle to rid Ireland of English domination.

There were many Anglo-Irish names amongst those working at the rediscovery of Ireland and simultaneously with their involvement in ancient Ireland came an impetus from the landlord class to make a 'New Ireland'. Horace Plunkett, John Shawe-Taylor and Josslyn Gore-Booth are representative of those Anglo-Irish who were eager to reform and put their theories into practice. It is too quickly assumed that reform in Ireland was a movement at grass-roots level, and that there was nothing but dead wood in the tree-tops; but reforming ideas were at large in a progressive section of the landlord class from early in the nineteenth century, their contacts in London and on the continent – particularly post-revolutionary France – ensuring that these ideas were refined and practical. William Thompson, who set up a co-operative system on his estate at Glandore in County Cork, became a propagandist for Robert Owen and an influence on Marx.

Ireland's economy was based on agriculture and it is difficult to see how the transition from English colony to the Republic of Ireland could have been made so effectively without Plunkett's vast and efficient network of co-operative creameries. Co-operative ideas had been introduced into Ireland early in the nineteenth century. Robert Owen had lectured in Dublin, and the experiments of Thompson and Vandeleur must have owed much to his inspiration. William Morris lectured in Dublin in 1886, the year of Gladstone's Home Rule Bill; his socialist co-operative ideas were widely reported and disseminated in pamphlets.

At this time, when Ireland was seen in England merely as the most primitive British province, progressive reformers emerged, like O'Connell, from this backwater to irritate the establishment with hectoring demands in Parliament. The progressive clique in Ireland included remarkable men from the Gore-Booth class whose ideas clearly foreshadow the eventual means of British withdrawal from Ireland. To the Gore-Booth girls, taking, as they did, the path through co-operation to socialism, the most important of these would have been Feargus O'Connor.

O'Connor's father, Roger, and his uncle Arthur had both been United Irishmen who took up arms against England in 1798, and Arthur became a General with Napoleon. Feargus, after training as a barrister and attending Trinity College Dublin, took part in the Reform agitation leading up to the Reform Act and was returned as MP for Cork in 1832. He began to associate with English radicals. He became the leader of the Chartists, owning and editing the Chartist paper the *Northern Star*. In 1846 he founded the National Land Company to purchase estates and let them to subscribers by ballot; he also formulated plans for peasant proprietorship fifty years before this was put into practice in Ireland. He became MP for Nottingham in 1847, but his behaviour was becoming increasingly disturbed and after a visit to America he was pronounced insane in June 1852. He died in 1855.

By the early 1890s, when Josslyn Gore-Booth was educating himself in socialism and co-operation, the movement in Ireland had steadied itself, lost many of its revolutionary overtones, and was in the process of being shown to be a workable system by Horace Plunkett and George Russell (Russell was the poet and theosophist AE), whose disciple Josslyn was.

Josslyn's career as a co-operator started in 1895 when he opened the Drumcliffe Dairy Society, the first co-operative creamery in Sligo and in 1896 he was heavily involved in the first Sligo conference of the Irish Agricultural Organisation Society. In 1902 he started the Sligo Manufacturing Society, organising 100 shareholders from all classes in Sligo to fund a shirt and clothing factory. He was a trained agronomist who used revolutionary farming techniques and his garden plants, particularly his Alpines, were celebrated.

Yet where his name survives it is in anecdotes of the kind that love to dwell on the eccentricities of the Anglo-Irish and he still raises laughs by his invention of a hollow cow from which to shoot wild geese and his successful pollination of a red primula called 'Red Hugh', as if his life had been spent alternately on all fours in his garden with a pollinating brush, and lying in a hollow cow clutching a shotgun.

Josslyn's choice of the name 'Red Hugh' is highly significant and declares his nationalist sympathies. Hugh Roe O'Donnell ('Red Hugh'), 1571?–1602, was lord of Tyrconnel and a leader of the last great attempt to defeat the Elizabethan English in Ireland. He destroyed Sligo Castle and other fortresses in 1595; invaded and plundered Connaught in 1597; with Hugh O'Neill, the Earl of Tyrone, he defeated the English at the Yellow Ford in 1598. He fled abroad after the defeat at the battle of Kinsale, and died, poisoned, in Spain in 1602.

Sir Henry's children were very aware of the Ireland that lay beneath them and they were especially conscious of the famous Irish family of poets, called O'Daly, who had lived at Lissadell before their time. Lissadell means 'the Fort of the Blind Man' and legend had it that the blind man was Muireadhach Albanach (Scots) O'Daly, brother of the poet Donnchadh Mór O'Daly, ancestor of the MacMhuireadhaigh (MacVurich) family, a famous line of bards who later flourished in Scotland. *Circa* 1213 Muireadhach O'Daly murdered an O'Donnell tax-gatherer at Lissadell to avenge an insult. Fleeing from O'Donnell retribution he retreated in stages via Thomond, Limerick, and Dublin to Scotland. During his time in Scotland he went on the Fifth Crusade in 1217 and his poems written on this crusade survived: now serving with the Scots, O'Daly still pines for Lissadell:

> How peaceful would my slumbers be
> In kind O'Conor's fair demesne,
> A poet in good company
> Couched upon Eire's rushes green.

When Constance was imprisoned after the rising she worked very hard at learning Irish, and her letters to Eva at this time refer to the O'Daly poet and his home at Lissadell.

In being aware of Irish Ireland the Gore-Booth children were unusual for their class, yet in some ways they fitted easily into it: Constance and Eva were both remarkably good horsewomen, and the whole family highly sociable, musical and convivial. It was not until they were in their mid-twenties that Josslyn and Eva began seriously to question landlordism, and Constance was a whole decade later than them in her revolt, joining Sinn Fein in Dublin after her marriage.

A large proportion of Anglo-Irish gentry in the nineteenth century lived in a sealed, self-satisfied world, where it was possible to live life through without once considering with guilt, or even curiosity, their position in a native society that was alien to them. For all their surface affability and disarming talent for warm personal relationships with those of inferior social status the Anglo-Irish lived in a closed world of blood relations and land-holding; just how Anglo-Irish society was closed we can sense from their disdain for those in trade, for the socially ambitious, and for the vulgarity of the 'low' church and common non-conformists.

That easy-going and bonhomous pair, Somerville and Ross, included a small, but give-away, remark in their tour of Wales *Beggars on Horseback* (1895). After bewilderedly failing to find any relatives in Wales ('*nobody* lives here') they damned Wales with the phrase 'the land of tin tabernacles' – as corrugated iron had been seized upon as the ideal building material for the intense constructive phase, in the mid-nineteenth century, of the chapels and meeting-houses of dissenting sects. The words 'tin tabernacle' were in use among the Anglo-Irish as a code word – Constance and Eva Gore-Booth used it in contracted form: 'tin tab'.

The Gore-Booths were admirable landlords, resident and deeply involved with their tenants and farms and the proper management of both. Old Lady Gore-Booth had toiled through the famine years of 1846–8 and consciousness of her duties made her a distinctly different type of mother to the womenfolk of absentee Irish landlords, living it up in London, or the more common type of English high-society lady.

Famine returned to Ireland in the winter of 1879–80, when Constance was twelve and Eva ten, and they worked with their parents at the distribution of food and clothing and nursing the sick. There can be no doubt that this experience of living in a famine district at such an impressionable age had an overwhelming effect on both girls. An alert social conscience and instant generosity was common to them both.

The evictions that came in the wake of the 1879–80 famine brought into being the Land League organised by Michael Davitt and Charles Stewart Parnell – who set themselves to dismantle the system of land-ownership in Ireland. Safely ensconced in their thousands of acres and convinced that they treated their tenants justly, indeed quite sure of their popularity, the Gore-Booths did not take the Land League seriously. Instead they found in it a source of amusement. In the same way they found the goings-on of the 'tin tab' brigade – the newly-found airs and graces, social and spiritual, of the labouring classes-cum-bourgeoisie, deeply funny.

In 1891 when the Land League and the middle classes could still be considered an amusing curiosity and not a real threat, Eva

wrote a burlesque sketch *A Daughter of Eve* or *Alphonso's Bride*.
Constance played the lead part of Fatima FitzHiggins and Eva
played Anne. In this sketch we can see the curiously zany sense of
humour that the sisters shared and their complete unawareness at
this time that their social position was seriously beleaguered. Eva
and Constance are on stage when there is a thunderous knocking
at the door. In their characters of Fatima and Anne, Eva and
Constance then discuss the nature of this 'something monstrous'
battering at the door of Anglo-Ireland.

Fatima:
  'If it was Gladstone you know he would talk.
  So would the Hon. member for Cork.'
Anne:
  'Yes, supposing it's Mr Parnell himself.
  He mightn't enjoy being put on the shelf.'
Fatima:
  'If it's Mr Healy he'll rage and shout
  No! We certainly won't let Timothy out.'
Anne:
  'Fatima! Now I have it
  I believe it's poor old Michael Davitt.'
Fatima:
  'If it's Mr Balfour, he daren't come out
  Because there's not one policeman about.'
Anne:
  'If it's Mr O'Brien there will be a row
  For they'll put him in prison if they catch him now.'
Fatima:
  'Yes, if it's Mr O'Brien you'd better beware
  For he's as cross as a polar bear.'
Anne:
  'If it's Potheen we'll drink it neat
  Old Irish whiskey is not to be beat.'

Clearly political consciousness had not developed in either girl;
they were aged twenty-three and twenty-one at this stage. The
burlesque includes many happy and deferential references to the
family with this curious variation on name-dropping: 'Either
Gore-Jones or Gore-Booth – Gore-Jones that's Gor-geous but

there's a terrible suggestion of the Salvation Army about Gore-Booth.'

Catherine Booth's work with the Salvation Army in the lower depths of London had not yet caught the imaginaton of either girl and the freakish element in their characters that led them to question and then discard the assumptions of their class is not at all obvious. In their class it was accepted that women could be characterful and active in certain spheres; yet from one of their grandmothers came an excess force of character that was to take Constance and Eva into spheres that women had not entered and to make them objects of horror and pity to their one-time fellows.

Eva's grandmother, Lady Hill, was the sister of Richard George Lumley, the ninth Earl of Scarbrough, and although she died when Eva was only nine years old this powerful old lady had a profound influence on her. The cult of strong female personality was marked in Gore-Booth ladies who, for as far back as we can trace them, flatly rejected the still-current notion that woman's identity is wholly sexual and subservient to man.

Aristocratic women lived on the periphery of their husband's and father's lives; from within the male preserves there issued stock reference books like Debrett's and Burke's Peerage where we see that a woman's identity in these pages was indeed contingent upon her bearing children. In Constance and Eva's day Burke's Peerage did not give the birth date of girl children as it did for boys. The first date connected with any female name is the date of her marriage.

The boys, listed and numbered one after another with their diamond symbols: ◆, and their offspring if married, are followed by their numbered and dotted: ●, sisters who appear simply as Christian names if unmarried, even if they are born before their brothers. Constance was the first-born of Sir Henry and Georgina Gore-Booth, yet she appears way down her generation list, after her baby brothers, in the Gore-Booth descent. At least she acquired a place in chronological history by marrying Casimir Dunin de Markievicz on 29 September 1900.

Even as late as the 1925 edition of Burke's Peerage, which was the year before Eva's death when she was an established and acclaimed poet and prose writer with many volumes published, she appears simply as: 2●Eva Selina. She is followed by:

3●Mabel, who again was rewarded with a date – 1 December 1900 – on her marriage to Charles Percival Foster.

Aristocratic women could become powerful and attain a certain amount of behind-the-scenes power by co-operating and playing life as a game with men, by their rules. It was a game that Eva refused to play from the beginning, and one that Constance rejected soon after her marriage. But their grandmother, and Lumley ladies as a breed, seem to have enjoyed the game and played it to perfection.

Baronets were small fry in the aristocratic world yet the Gore-Booths were expert operators on the marriage market and we find Eva and Constance related to the topmost ranks of British society, both the English and the Irish peerage, by their father's marriage to Georgina Hill. Her mother, Frances Charlotte Arabella Lumley, sister of Richard George, Earl of Scarbrough and Viscount Lumley of Waterford in the Irish peerage, married Colonel Charles John Hill on 8 March 1836, thus entering history by Burke's definition, and bore him children. Colonel Hill died in 1867 and Lady Hill decided to join the household of her favourite daughter, Georgina, by this time married to Henry Gore-Booth.

A disagreement as to the altitude of Lady Hill's rank must have arisen at some stage in her social career (some young whipper-snapper must have tried to precede her into dinner) for Burke's tell us: 'This lady and her sisters were granted the precedence of earl's daughters.'

Eva's grandmother's brother, the ninth Earl, married Frederica Drummond, niece of the Earl of Perth, and this pair triumphed dynastically with their four daughters who made brilliant marriages. By them Eva's grandmother became Aunt to (1) the fourth Lady Bolton, (2) the fourth Countess of Bradford, (3) the Marchioness of Zetland (the Zetlands were Lord and Lady Lieutenant of Ireland between 1889–92), and (4) the Countess Grosvenor. This last was young Sibell Mary who married first the eldest son of the Duke of Westminster but second, and most important for the Irish connection, on 7 February 1887 the Right Hon. George Wyndham, PC, MP for Dover and mastermind of the Wyndham Acts of the early years of this century that began the transfer, by purchase, of Irish land from the landlord to the tenant. George Wyndham was Chief Secretary at the Irish Office from 1900–5.

So when, in 1916, Constance had so far revolted against her class as to take up arms against England and her husband quipped that she could not possibly be sentenced to death as half of Debrett's would have to go into mourning, this was not a light jest. Constance's life was saved by special pleading in high places – not that she wished it to be saved – by Eva's use of their family connections. Asquith's secretary was a friend of a relation.

Eva quite deliberately left her family and her class and made a satisfying new life for herself, very much in the public eye. We can know little of her early life in Ireland and what were the momentous workings in her mind that caused her to reject permanent engagement with men as a way of life, and to reject enclosure within her class as her proper station. After her death Esther Roper, in clearing Eva's bedroom and ordering the personal papers there, found a manuscript called 'The Inner Life of a Child' and this does give us a picture of Eva as a child in the remote West of Ireland.

Eva was six when her grandfather, Sir Robert Gore-Booth, died at Lissadell at the end of December 1876. At what should have been a joyful and high-spirited Christmas time she was perplexed by the descent of gloom upon the household, the disappearance of her grandfather and the ceremonials surrounding his burial. Unlike many of the Gore-Booth men who were of the hugely physical and adventurous type, not given to art, Sir Robert had been a musician and gifted horticulturalist; many of his descendants were to be gardeners and plantsmen of distinction. He was a kind man and admired by his tenants for his generosity and open-handed dealings.

It is likely that the event that most disturbed Eva, whose dreams were made dreadful by visions of coffins, was the sight of her grandfather's coffin being carried by relays of tenants from Lissadell where they had gathered in a huge silent crowd, to the church at Drumcliffe, three miles distant.

She took herself away from this scene to a hiding place:

Very intimately connected with the inner life of my childhood was a little wood, that had once held a garden, and that was now so isolated from the world that it was called by us children St. Helena. A great many snowdrops grew among the hemlock roots, and here and there the formal lines of white in the tangled grass pointed out the place where there had once been flower beds . . .

Eva continues to talk of herself in the third person.

> On that January day she had realised clearly and practically the fact of death . . . she gradually became conscious of a strong intuitive feeling . . . a sense of something swift and free, of some life in the world beyond the senses . . . she knew . . . that the event was quite close to her and was explaining itself to her in an unmistakable intimate way . . . she put it into clumsy words that half shocked herself – 'Now I understand it all, and it's delightful to die, and wonderful to think of anybody being dead.' She was conscious of a vast comradeship, of unseen hands held out to her, of kindness . . .

Then her intensity of understanding left her 'and she went back to the dark child's world puzzled, and with a heavy heart'.

Three years later her adored grandmother died. Esther came to know how much Eva had loved her grandmother through Eva's stories: 'She was devoted to her grandmother Lady Hill and was absolutely happy when the latter read or talked to her, especially about religion.' On the death of Lady Hill, Eva, only nine years old, became obsessed by death and physical decay and so distressed that she was only calmed by feeling her grandmother's presence with her. Again, in *The Inner Life of a Child*, Eva refers to herself in the third person:

> When she was nine her grandmother died, and someone told her she had gone to heaven. This idea did not touch her, it seemed vague and unreal . . . she became very morbid over the idea of death. Her head became full of gruesome fancies which she thought of constantly, and often she used to lie in bed at nights, and touch her own hands, and wonder if it were possible that some day they would be a mass of decay. She became for a time obsessed by the physical idea of death, and a coffin was specially horrible to her; the idea of the absence of light and air filled her with unspeakable terror . . . but one evening a new happiness came to her. 'We children were sent to bed early and it was broad daylight.' Without any warning the child became conscious that a 'door had opened in the air', and

that her grandmother was standing beside her . . . the child, who in theory was terrified of ghosts, had no thought of fear, nor did she even think it strange, she was simply delighted to be with her again.

For many years Eva continued to see her grandmother and, Eva wrote, 'it was many years before she ever dreamt of questioning or doubting the actual presence of the dead woman'. When she came to doubt and to think of attributing these manifestations to her own imagination she tested her powers of imagination by trying to will a window-blind, drawn down so that it obscured the lawns and the sea, out of existence. On failing to do this Eva concluded:

She gradually lost a practical belief in the power of the imagination to materialize what has no existence, and grew to look upon the faculty that goes by that name as simply a subtler and keener perception of things that are really there.

Eva had telepathic communication with her old nurse, and knew that she could infallibly bring the nurse to her simply by willing it, at whatever hour of night. She dreamed the death of this nurse on the night of the event, when the nurse was two years retired from the household at Lissadell, and far distant.

This very early deliberate confrontation with loss, death and decay made the child Eva cool, thoughtful and acutely apprecia-tive of natural beauty. Precisely the same events, the death of beloved grandparents, were brushed aside by Constance and left her unmarked. Eva was never to display any of the passionate frenzy of her sister after she had found her 'cause' in Ireland. A passage in *The Inner Life of a Child* shows that Eva was literally an Apollonian child:

Then there are the revelations of human vision and labour – the poem that one reads for the first time, the words never heard before that thunder through one's brain and waken echoes in the caves of one's remotest consciousness. The sudden uncom-prehended beauty that stares one in the face . . . . The child remembers once opening a parcel in the cold dark hours of a December morning. In those days she had seen very little of the world, and nothing of the beauty of art. Out of a bundle of brown paper and straw emerged a face, a beautiful white gleaming face, such a face as she had never seen in her conscious life; and yet in a moment a mad struggling throng of associations, of dreams, of ideas jostled together in her mind. The door of all the mysteries opened in the air and there and then she flung herself down on her knees by the schoolroom table, and prayed with all her heart to a cast of Apollo . . .

Fifty years later, just before her death, Eva was to repeat the very first spiritual question she formulated as a child. She is describing herself:

dreadfully puzzled by the sequences of life and all those things that make up the working compromise of the spirit and the flesh . . . . In the midst of the confusion which surrounds our first pitiful attempts to unite the warring elements, it is no wonder the child's spirit thrills in response to those magnificent words that seem to hold the whole secret of life: 'Before Abraham was, I am.' This is the eternal and only answer to the first question of awakened consciousness – 'What happens when I die, what happened before I was born?'

What Eva calls the 'magnificent words' of Christ were spoken after his defence of the woman taken in adultery: 'He that is without sin among you, let him first cast a stone at her,' when the Jews cross-examined him as to his exact relationship with Abraham: 'Thou art not yet fifty years old, and hast thou seen Abraham?' (St John, 9).

Eva's girlhood at Lissadell was made endurable by her governesses, particularly the long-suffering Miss Noel (christened Squidge by Constance) who grounded Eva in Latin and Greek and introduced her to the art and literature of Italy with which Eva fell head over heels in love for life. Squidge came to Lissadell when Eva was twelve and became an intimate friend. Of Eva in 1882 Miss Noel wrote to Esther:

Eva was a very fair, fragile-looking child, most unselfish and gentle with the general look of a Burne-Jones or Botticelli angel. As she was two years younger than Constance, and always so delicate, she had been, I think, rather in the background and a little lonely mentally, but music was a great joy to her . . . . We were a great deal at Lissadell with Mabel, her younger sister, while Lady Gore-Booth and Constance were in London, after the latter 'came out', and we were very happy reading Dante together: Eva was of course presented in her turn and a good deal admired but society of the fashionable kind did not, I think, ever appeal much to her . . .

She made her first extensive travels in 1894 with her father to the West Indies and America and in the following year she was with her mother at Bayreuth for the Wagner Festival and then in Italy. She suffered an 'alarming illness' in Venice and was instructed by doctors to spend the next winter by the Mediterranean, and in carrying out this instruction Eva met Esther Roper and boldly stepped out of her seclusion to join her friend. She was twenty-six.

She did not care too much for masculinity in general and she made none of the connections with dashing young men that might have been expected. But she was not cold towards men and was most certainly attractive. Yeats was smitten by her. It is her poetry that reveals her calm rejection of 'masculinity'; from her teens she persistently connected the masculine with possessiveness, domination and the mechanical – the 'iron fort' of materialism – and she connected the feminine with intuition, nature and an ecstatic peace:

> Men have got their pomp and pride.
> All the green world is on our side.

She could see no just reason for her father's overlordship of a huge estate and such numbers of poor people, and though her poem *The Land to the Landlord* was written after leaving Lissadell it must surely be one of the most remarkable protests from an Irish landlord's daughter on behalf of Ireland:

> You hug to your soul a handful of dust
> And you think the round world your sacred trust . . .
>
> O the bracken waves and the foxgloves flame
> And none of them ever has heard your name . . .
> Near and dear is the curlews cry,
> You are a stranger passing by.

Though you are king of the rose and the wheat
Not for you, not for you is the bog-myrtle sweet
Though you are lord of all the long grass
The hemlock bows not her head as you pass.

The poppies would flutter amongst the corn
Even if you had never been born,
With your will or without your will
The ragweed can wander over the hill.

Down there in the bog where the plovers call
You are but an outcast after all
Over your head the sky gleams blue
Not a cloud or a star belongs to you.

> (*Complete Poems of Eva Gore-Booth*, p. 238.
> None of her work is now in print.)

In another poem, *Heredity*, Eva does not once mention her father but muses over her mother. Had the parents of the poet read *Heredity* they would have been chilled:

There is one thing I know
About life, and thought and art –
That my soul did not grow,
Out of my mother's heart.

Clearly Eva did not 'connect' with her mother as she did with her grandmother:

But my spirit did not arise
Out of my mother's will.

She was obviously at odds with the example of femininity set her by her mother.

But my soul is not the child
Of my mother's brain.

The idea of soul, and its reincarnation, was to fascinate Eva throughout her life, from her first discussions with her grandmother.

These things I know because
In Life, and Thought and Art
The soul obeys strange laws
That break the heart.
(*Complete Poems of Eva Gore-Booth*, p. 294.)

Eva was to take a most unusual road through life – refusing to conform to the habits of both her class and her sex, she would have neither of the two roles available for her. She would not be subsumed by marriage and she had seen what became of the maiden aunt in Anglo-Irish great houses. Her father's sister Augusta was one. An invalid by the time of Yeats' visit she struck him as the strongest-willed person living at Lissadell, 'mostly invisible but is always more or less behind the scenes like an iron claw'. In less opulent households the maiden aunt was little more than a companionable, very familiar, upper servant.

In Martin Ross's letters references to 'Selina' who was always at hand in the Martin family home, Ross in County Galway, doing things like preparing meals, rooms for guests and changing beds, might lead us to think that this was a servant, but she was Martin's elder sister, unable to escape from Ross, having no talents to live by.

A route that avoided both marriage and her turning down the long side-road of maiden-aunthood was irresistible to Eva. Edward Carpenter, when writing of the vitalising effect upon other women of early women suffragists referred both to married and unmarried middle-class women when he wrote of their life as 'tragic in its emptiness'. It is now much better understood that psychic well-being has an overriding effect on physical well-being but it is still remarkable that Eva – diagnosed by doctors as close to death in 1895 – by her connection with Esther Roper and the cause of women's suffrage came back to life and hard work for a further thirty years.

By 1895, the year in which Eva's medical diagnosis was suspected consumption, she had developed into a serious thinker, long before Constance. She was troubled by class inequalities, deprivation, poverty and the low status of women. When she met Esther Roper for the first time she was able not only to talk about these things but to join an organisation and work physically for a cause. This involved leaving her family and Lissadell which she did by an instantaneous decision, but her family were alarmed and dismayed at the thought of the adored and gentle Eva living and working in Manchester with, as her chosen companion, the daughter of a factory hand who was distinctly 'tin tab'. To them it must have seemed Eva was obeying a strange and very unnatural law that broke their hearts.

CHAPTER 2

THE BACKGROUND AND CHILDHOOD OF ESTHER ROPER

Miss Esther Roper, BA, was a most unusual woman whose chief personal characteristic seems to have been self-effacement. She never revealed anything of her family and background and her fellow-suffragists never throw light on her in their papers and memoirs with a kindly personal remark. She is just there – 'Miss Roper' – greatly respected as the mainstay of the women's suffrage movement in Manchester in the 1890s with her mission to unionise women industrial workers. This was an entirely new and revolutionary aim in the suffrage movement whose leaders and organisers had tended to come from Liberal and moneyed classes and to operate in that sphere only. What kind of upbringing could account for Esther Roper's new approach to suffrage organisation?

When Esther Roper was born on 4 August 1868 at Lindow, Chorley, Cheshire, 'Occupation of father' on her birth certificate was briskly filled in as 'Clergyman' which would seem to provide Esther with a comfortable cultivated middle-class background – we would hardly expect a girl from such a background to take women's suffrage as her life-work let alone organising unions for women workers. But a closer look at the Reverend Edward Roper shows us how fluid and receptive the English class system had become when industrial wealth could hold its own against inherited wealth. The Reverend Roper was a very early riser in the dawn of 'upward social mobility', a poor boy from a broken home who left school at eleven to work as a factory hand. Edward Roper struggled out of his Manchester slum via his

Sunday School at St Jude's in Ancoats to become a missionary with the Church Missionary Society (CMS) in Africa.

He became sufficiently confident to describe himself as 'gentleman' on his marriage certificate when he married Annie Craig, the daughter of an Irish immigrant to Manchester, at Douglas in the Isle of Man in August 1867. Casting a slight blight upon that brave 'gentleman' Edward Roper's rectitude set down, two entries to the right, the name and occupation of his drunken wastrel of a father: 'Thomas Roper, warehouseman', who lived apart from his wife after burdening her with a large family. Annie Craig had been born to her Irish parents in Manchester shortly after they had left Ireland in 1842 and she insisted on registering herself as 'Irish' for the rest of her life although Manchester-born. Esther Roper, then, was half Irish and of completely working-class stock, and she may well have been the first woman from such a background to earn a BA. Although her working-class origins have been obscured by her own reticence and later historians' assumptions that she was a typical middle-class do-gooder, they were certainly known to her contemporaries and colleagues in Manchester, and the reason for her interest in working-class women and her very great success in working with them and organising for them is now apparent.

Esther Roper was educated through the charity of the Church Missionary Society after her father died when she was nine. Her father's struggle to better himself, although it did provide her with a sound education in later years, made Esther's childhood grim and impersonal. The story of her parents' time in Africa and the organisation of the CMS in evangelising abroad and education at home is interesting and explains much of the development of Esther's character: self-sufficient, unemotional, very competent and with only a theoretical understanding of the words 'family' and 'love'.

The Church Missionary Society suffered such a severe shortage of volunteers for missionary work during the 1850s that it started a campaign to attract likely boys to the missions, through its Sunday Schools and the Juvenile Church Missionary Association. One Sunday in St Jude's, Edward Roper duly read an advertisement in the *C.M. Juvenile Instructor*: 'Wanted, more missionaries. Do our young friends ever pray that God would direct the course of some of them into the missionary field?' In his mid-teens Edward Roper had been a rather unpleasant and aggressive character who had been reformed by contact first with a scripture reader called Mr Taylor, whose early death devastated the boy, and later with the Rev. J. MacCartie who came as Rector to St Jude's in 1857. Struck by the advertisement he cut it out and pasted it inside the lid of the box in which he kept his Sunday clothes. His fellow parishioners, unconvinced by his change in character, looked askance at his ambition to become a missionary. The Reverend MacCartie knew that Edward's parents lived apart and that the mother struggled to bring up a large family in utter poverty. Edward's wages were of great importance to her and the Reverend MacCartie's sympathies were all with Mrs Roper whom he described as 'excellent, hard working and afflicted'. Edward was advised against leaving home. This had no effect, his mind was set; after months of pleading from Edward, the Reverend MacCartie agreed to put Edward's case to his mother. She heard the Rector out and then briefly replied: 'If the Lord will have him, he mun go.'

MacCartie later published a memoir of Edward Roper, after Roper's early death, as an account of his remarkable achievements in Africa. In this memoir he quite frankly discusses the fact that by becoming a missionary Edward Roper knew that he was bettering himself socially. It is a point frequently made in CMS publications and Edward Roper must often have read pamphlets like an 'Appeal to Sunday School teachers on behalf of missions':

> I look at your influence prospectively. Sunday school children often rise in society . . . many will, without doubt, become respectable tradespeople, will increase their contributions as their means increase and, in due time, inoculate their children with the missionary spirit. Some will become the ministers and missionaries of the next generation, and some, in the progress of colonization may go to infuse that spirit into the infant empires of the coming age.

These ideas captivated Edward Roper and gave him a route by which to make himself as different as possible from his father; his Christian belief was quite sincere but still, MacCartie tells us, he himself was the only believer in the sincerity and singleness of purpose of Edward Roper – 'the curate, the Scripture readers, the Sunday school teachers, all gave him credit for a mere ambition to step out of his rank'. Charles Kingsley's working-class hero Alton

Locke only had one route of escape from his slum, by becoming a missionary.

Although we may find laughable Edward Roper's do-it-yourself transformation from uneducated factory-hand to 'gentleman' Africa proved him to be a man of great natural intelligence, of intense application and the utmost sangfroid – qualities he passed on to his eldest child, and all qualities that could be quietly self-contained and not obvious to the casual observer.

The Church Missionary Society showed a remarkable confidence in the young uneducated men that they plucked from the provinces. After only a few months training at the CMS college at Islington, in the summer of 1859 Edward Roper sailed for the Yoruba mission, in what is now Nigeria, having been appointed a lay catechist. After three years' work at the Abeokuta mission Edward Roper was taken into captivity by the Ibadans when they destroyed the town of Ijaye where he was stationed. The full-scale tribal war between the Egbas (the Abeokuta tribe) and the Ibadans went on for some years and Edward Roper spent three years in captivity; his first mission in Africa from 1859–65 proved him very adaptable, perceptive and receptive in the most awful circumstances. Of major importance to his success as a missionary was the speed with which he learned to preach in, and later to speak, Yoruba. He was infuriated by the standard practice at that time of a halting, phrase by phrase translation being made by a native interpreter, and set himself to master Yoruba, an extraordinary task for a young man who up until that time had only expressed himself in Lancashire dialect. Yoruba speakers, both native and older missionaries, were impressed by Edward Roper's Yoruba. As proof that he was indeed an exceptional student of this language Bishop Crowther, the first native Bishop in Africa, who met Edward Roper during this first period in Africa, chose him to supervise the dictionary of the Yoruba language when it was going through the press in England. Bishop Crowther had spent many years enslaved in the Yoruba country. He had translated the New Testament into Yoruba by 1861; he was ordained in 1843, and made Bishop in 1864, the year before Edward Roper's release from captivity.

The young missionary's response to primitive African society – at this time slavery and ritual sacrifice were still everyday occurrences – was remarkably open-minded and candidly set down in a series of *Tracts* published by the CMS to educate the church-going public – whose donations supported the missions – with a general picture of Africa and the mission work there. These little tracts were illustrated with woodcuts showing the young missionary about his work. As someone who, only a year before, had been a factory-hand in a Manchester glass works, the experience of for example finding a fellow-villager's severed head in a basket or having a furious public exchange with a priestess coated in red-ochre and wearing only a loin-cloth should have been mentally unsettling, but Edward Roper's nerve was rock-steady.

Conspicuous in these tracts is Edward Roper's esteem of women, of whatever colour, and his recognition of their domestic enslavement:

> Domestic slavery still exists . . . and will cease only in propor-
> tion to the spread of Christianity and lawful commerce . . .
> slavery is a dreadful thing if we judge by its fruits. I knew a
> woman in one town who was obliged to bribe her husband not
> to sell her and her child, because she was his slave as well as his
> wife, the mother being a slave, according to native law her child
> also was a slave, and both could be sold at the master's will . . .

Edward Roper's sympathy with the native women took a very practical form. He had no qualms about intervention:

> In another town a boy called Adegum was about to be taken as
> a bond servant, for the small sum of three pounds, which his
> mother owed; had I not lent her the money to pay her debt, he
> would have become a slave . . .

Perhaps because as a group the women were more accustomed to patience and listening many of Edward Roper's first converts were women and he had the horrible experience of seeing what the tribe could exact in the way of punishment on such converts:

> the relatives and friends of the convert are greatly alarmed.
> They call in the priestess, who comes, and at first tries
> persuasion, this fails. She tries threatening. She is now very
> angry; and though an angry priest is much to be feared, an
> angry priestess is to be feared more . . . . The pressure put on

the convert increases, fetters, starvation, whipping . . . . At last, in anger one says 'Kill her, and be done with it.'

Edward Roper's experiences during his first mission were a great strain on him mentally and physically which he had to endure alone. He returned home to Manchester at Easter 1865, gaunt and still in very poor health after his three years' imprisonment. At a church function in the neighbouring parish of St James, Collyhurst, he met his future wife, Annie Craig, a strong-minded and devout young woman who was ready and willing to give her life to mission work in Africa.

By his work in Africa Edward Roper did indeed make a great change in his own status. As soon as he returned to England he began to study for his ordination, and also began to give his immensely popular series of lectures on Africa, illustrated with 'magic-lantern' slides. He became a celebrity on the CMS circuit within a year of his return. 1867 was to be a triumphant year: he was married in August and ordained the following month. The young Rev. and Mrs Roper spent the first year of their marriage in a rather peripatetic way, on 'supply duty', waiting for their new posting to Africa.

It was while the Rev. Roper was working as assistant to the Rev. James Consterdine of Alderley Edge that his first child was born at Lindow, Chorley. Rev. Roper had come to the attention of the Bishop of Carlisle, Dr Waldegrave, when he was visiting Raughton Head and it was this great dignitary who baptised the baby Esther Gertrude Roper. The Bishop took a great interest in Edward Roper and chaired a lecture that he gave on African missions. The Bishop gave his frank reaction to Rev. MacCartie who tells us in his memoir that there were:

such graphic details of African life, such interesting traits of African character, so many proverbs indicating African thought and judgement were interspersed with a clear and well arranged narrative of the Mission work, that the good Bishop after the lecture said to me that he had never in his life been so intensely interested, nor had he ever heard anything which made him so able to understand the African character, he said. 'Such a lecture presents an entire confutation of the theories of the Anthropologists. A people such as these Africans, with such proverbs, are capable of high cultivation; their hearts are fashioned like ours.'

Obviously Edward Roper was humane to an unusual degree for his time and it comes as rather a shock to discover that baby Esther was attached to a wet-nurse and left behind with her Irish grandparents in Manchester at the age of three months while her parents sailed off for an unknown number of years to Africa.

There were sound reasons for leaving Esther at home. The missionary societies had from the very beginning accepted the service of women starting way back in 1815 with three ladies from Clifton. The CMS in its first hundred years sent out 2,003 missionaries, 485 of these being women. The wonderful stamina and life work of women like Mary Slessor were celebrated, but these were the achievements of the unmarried. The missionary societies learned to be careful of married women after the disastrous expedition known as the 'Helmore-Price'.

In the year that Edward Roper set to work at Abeokuta the London Missionary Society sent a party of two missionaries' families into Central Africa, the Helmores with four children, and the recently-married Roger Price and his wife Isabella Slater, who was already pregnant. The wives were enthusiastic and determined not to be left behind. The men were ignorant of the desert, but were convinced that by taking women and children with them they would more easily win the confidence and interest of the natives. The natives in fact relieved them of necessities and the party got into difficulties at the end of 1859 and was lost in the desert. Mrs Price bore a girl child. In all, of the party of a dozen in two wagons, nine died of fever and thirst in the Kalahari: Mr Helmore, both missionaries' wives, three children and three native aides. Roger Price, a huge, burly man, was found in rags, wandering deliriously, accompanied by two Helmore orphans.

When the Ropers were posted to their new duties in Africa the interior was closed against Yoruba missionaries, but the fact that Mrs. Roper was again pregnant ensured that they were stationed in the coastal town of Lagos. Their joint work there was to found a Female Institution – a corrugated iron building; the 'tin tab' had reached Africa – for the education of Native Christian girls which was opened on 1 May 1869. Annie Craig Roper wrote an article about this Institution that was published in the *Church Missionary Gleaner*. Annie Roper clearly matched her husband in her esteem of native Africans and their womenfolk. She describes how the coming of trade and the establishment of the missions brought about change in Lagos 'which up to that time had been the principal slave mart on the West coast of Africa. . . .' Day schools were taught by natives who had been trained for the purpose. The Ropers' unusual idea was this: 'Something must be done to give a good education to the elder girls, who would be the future wives and mothers of the educated native gentlemen.' These were quite revolutionary thoughts for their day in black Africa. The Institution flourished, Annie Roper herself teaching English there. The Ropers were well-pleased with the success of the Institution: 'Many of those who enter the Institution become the wives of educated natives, and others marry native teachers . . . the missionaries know well that the children of the next generation will be what the mothers of this make them.'

His Excellency Captain Strahan, the Governor of Lagos, took great pleasure in the progress of the Institution and presented prizes to the pupils on open-days. The Reverend and Mrs Roper had their place in colonial society in Lagos, but Mrs Roper's pregnancy gave her grave ill-health and immediate return to England was advised. Esther's sister, Annie Justina, was born on board ship two days off Lagos. She died at five months old.

Edward Roper resumed his duties in England again as an assistant deputising for absent or sick clergymen. During this time before they returned to Lagos in 1872, Annie Roper lived with Esther at her parents' home, Fountain Villas, off Cheetham Hill in Central Manchester. It was a crowded household, and we are told a great deal about it by the 1871 census. Head of the household, George Craig, sixty years old at this stage, features interestingly on the Ropers' marriage certificate under 'father/ occupation' as 'Inspector'. Slater's Directory reveals him to have been an Inspector of Nuisances (and Hackney Carriages) whose office was in the back quarters of the City Hall.

Not all poor Irish immigrants in Manchester made a success of their new lives, but George Craig shepherded his family success- fully into the English lower-middle classes. He had six children, three of each; his sons were shippers' clerks and he kept his unmarried daughters at home. His eldest daughter Sarah had been born in Ireland and at the age of 31 was still unmarried. Annie Craig was the only one of his children to be married in 1871. There was one domestic servant, an eighteen year old from Crumpsall, called Elizatha [*sic*] Johnson.

Clearly Esther could not be left here indefinitely while her parents were in Africa and before the Ropers left for Lagos in

1872 they had found the solution. Esther Gertrude Roper was admitted to the Church Missionary Children's Home in Highbury on 14 October 1872. She was four. Her school was a free boarding school for the children of missionaries. In the next five years she saw her parents infrequently at intervals, one of more than two years.

During her school holidays it seems that Esther was posted to Manchester, as she had no relatives in the south, and in 1875 she was in the company of her parents in the summer holidays when they bought a house in Manchester. Edward Roper's health was by now permanently broken down and the CMS decided to employ him in England rather than risk sending him on any further missions. Mrs Roper was scarcely in any better case; a third girl child, Florence, died of typhoid late in 1875 when she was again pregnant. Reginald Roper was born in January of 1876.

Despite his poor health Edward Roper travelled about the North of England with his magic lantern giving his celebrated lectures on heathen lands. He was very well-informed on satanism and idolatry and fascinated by cult and fetish objects which he illustrated in his magic lantern slides. It is to be supposed that Esther heard her father give these lectures. The Reverend Mac-Cartie tells us of the 'audiences of young people, sometimes in thousands' who flocked to hear him.

Annie Roper told the Reverend MacCartie about her husband's last months in Manchester. How he stoically tramped through fog and rain despite frequent inflammation of the lungs. On many of these walks to and from churches or lecture halls we see that 'our little daughter was with him', on walks of several miles. Clearly Esther was a sturdy infant used to long tramps. His last lecture, Annie told Rev. MacCartie, was on 'Central Africa, with dissolving views'. After giving the lecture he collapsed with pleurisy. His doctor had to administer morphia, then, Annie wrote: 'our little girl, who had often tended him in his illnesses, though only eight years old, read the fourteenth chapter of St John to him, at his request, and afterwards prayed with him'. During the following afternoon Edward Roper began to talk in Yoruba, but in a few moments of clarity before his death he spoke directly to Annie in Lancashire dialect.

Completely without means the widow had to rely on the Church Missionary Society for a pension and for the education of

continued on p. 40

Obituary

THE CHURCH MISSIONARY GLEANER. Apr. 1877

THE LATE REV. E. ROPER

Few of the younger missionaries whom it has pleased God to take away in the prime of life have left a more fragrant memory behind them than Edward Roper. Though not forty years of age when he died, his life had been marked by "changes and chances" above the average; and if the result of this has been that his name is not specially associated with any one important missionary enterprise, the variety of his experiences, and his skill in utilising them in God's service made his career one of no common interest and usefulness.

Edward Roper was born of humble parentage at Horwich, in Lancashire. He left school before he was eleven years old to work for his living, but continued to attend Sunday-school at St. Jude's, Manchester, and joined a mutual improvement class connected with it. He was then but a thoughtless lad, but the death of his teacher brought the words he had heard in class solemnly to his mind, and thus became the starting-point in his spiritual life. In 1857, when the Rev. J. MacCartie,* now Vicar of Greatham, became Rector of St. Jude's, he found Edward Roper a Sunday-school teacher, and secretary of the Juvenile Church Missionary Association.

About this time there appeared on the back of the *C.M. Juvenile Instructor* the following appeal:— "Wanted, more missionaries. Do our young friends ever pray that God would direct the course of some of them into the missionary field?" Roper cut out these words, and pasted them inside the lid of the box where he kept his Sunday clothes, that they might meet his eye continually. Home difficulties were in the way; but he wrote anonymously to Mr. Venn, then Hon. Sec. of the C.M.S., for advice, requesting an answer on the cover of the *Instructor*. The reply

---

* We take the facts of Mr. Roper's early life from an interesting account by Mr. MacCartie, which appeared in the C.M. *Juvenile Instructor* for December last. A fuller memoir, also from his pen, will appear shortly.

THE LATE REV. E. ROPER

appeared in due course; "Commit your way to God in earnest prayer; inform your parents, and consult your minister." Roper accordingly went to Mr. MacCartie, who advised delay, but some months afterwards agreed to speak to "his excellent, hard-working, and afflicted mother." Her brief reply was, "*If the Lord will have him, he mun go.*" He was accepted by the Society, and received some further training in a "supplemental class" attached at that time to the College at Islington, after which he and a fellow student, Mr. George Jefferies, were appointed to the Yoruba Mission as lay catechists.

The two friends sailed together in November, 1859. Roper was stationed at Abeokuta, and Jefferies at Ibadan. Those were the days when seven or eight European missionaries were not thought too many to divide between these great African towns. *Now*, the whole work is done by African pastors—so great has been the advance. But long years of trial were then approaching. In 1860, war broke out between the Egbas (the Abeokuta tribe) and the Ibadans, and was carried on in a desultory fashion year after year, desolating the country, and terribly hindering missionary work. In March, 1862, the town of Ijaye was utterly destroyed by the Ibadan army. A little flock of Christians there, the fruits of the Rev. A. Mann's labours, were carried into captivity; and Mr. Roper, who was in charge at the time, was made prisoner by a war chief notorious for his cruelty. He was taken to Ibadan, and a large ransom was demanded for him; but Mr. Hinderer's influence with the chiefs procured permission for him to live in the Mission-house, on condition that he did not leave the town until the ransom was paid. Thus the two old fellow-students were again under one roof. But not for long: within six months Mr. Jefferies succumbed to the severe privations which the scarcity produced by the war brought on the Mission party. (His grave-stone is seen in the picture of Kudeti Church, in the GLEANER of December, 1875.)

For three years Mr. Roper was shut up in Ibadan with Mr. and Mrs. Hinderer, sharing the sufferings so touchingly described in the memoir of the latter (*Seventeen Years in the Yoruba Country*), but taking diligent part in the care of the flock gathered by their faithful teaching from among the heathen. When at length, in 1865, through the energy of Captain (now Sir John) Glover, a way was made for their escape, he returned with them to England.

Mr. Roper now resumed his studies, and in September, 1867, he was ordained at Brighton by Bishop Beckles, of Sierra Leone, who was then in England. In the following year he returned to Africa, and received priest's orders at Sierra Leone, at the hands of the same Bishop. The interior of Yoruba being now closed against European missionaries, he was stationed at Lagos; and it was he and Mrs. Roper who were chiefly instrumental in starting the Female Institution for the education of Native Christian girls, which was opened on May 1st, 1869, as related by Mrs. Roper herself in the GLEANER of October, 1875. Only for a few months, however, were they permitted to carry on this good work, for Mrs. Roper's health suddenly broke down, and they had to return home.

In 1872, Mr. Roper again went out to Lagos, and was in successive charge of the Bread Fruit Church, the Faji Church, and the Training Institution. In December, 1873, he undertook, with Mr. Maser, a journey of inquiry into the little known countries east of Lagos, which resulted in the establishment by Mr. Hinderer of the Leke and Ondo Missions referred to in our February number. His visit also, shortly after, to Abeokuta, prepared the way for Mr. Townsend's return thither after seven years' exclusion. But in March, 1874, failure of health again compelled his return to England—as it proved, finally.

The last two years and a half were a constant struggle of a vigorous mind and an earnest spirit against bodily weakness. Mr. Roper threw himself heart and soul into that important branch of C.M.S. work, the maintaining of missionary interest in our own country. As a preacher and speaker for the Society he was most untiring and very acceptable; and many are the juvenile associations, especially in the north of England, which have been stirred up by his magic-lantern lectures. With what brightness and vividness he could describe the scenes and people he had lived amongst in Africa, the readers of the GLEANER know from the interesting series of articles in our last year's volume—cut short, alas! by his fatal illness.

Edward Roper died in harness. On Sunday, October 8th, he preached at St. James's, Collyhurst, Manchester, the parish in which the Rev. C. T. Wilson, of the Nyanza Mission, had been curate. On the Monday he addressed a missionary meeting in Cheshire, and on the Tuesday gave a lecture on Central Africa at Collyhurst. Referring on this latter occasion to the death of Mr. J. Robertson at Zanzibar, the news of which had just arrived, he exclaimed, "Who knows who may be the next?" He went home utterly worn out, and stricken with inflammation of the lungs; and on the Saturday evening he entered into rest. Almost his last words were, "I have been the chief of sinners, but I have a great Saviour, and all is peace."

her children. We may wonder how much Esther absorbed from her father when he died so young. Some of his writings were edited and published in a volume called *Christian Assurance* by the Reverend MacCartie, his CMS *Tracts* are very vivid, and Esther must have retained some memory of his public lectures. The qualities of internationalism and marked equalitarianism noted in her father, were developed in a feminist way in the daughter.

Often as a child would she have heard these sentiments:

As the consequence of your labours, and in answer to your prayers, the world is beginning to feel its destitution and its misery, and the loud cry is heard for help from millions who are perishing from lack of knowledge . . . . You have the power of *numbers*. Nearly two million of minds are under your influence, and indirectly as many more. You have *unity*, while every section of the Christian church has been rent by divisions . . . (A Sunday School Union address by Thomas Thompson).

If we were searching for early influences on the mind of the first successful women's suffrage union organiser we must not overlook that potent little phrase 'the power of numbers', a power that Esther Roper was first to mobilise in the women's suffrage movement.

Esther was to inherit no family money. On his death-bed her father told his doctor that he had only one regret – 'Leaving Annie and the children to battle with the world' – and he fretted over the fact that he was leaving his widow and children unprovided for. The doctor tried to comfort Edward Roper with the thought of God: 'Oh, yes . . . I can leave them in His hands. He will provide for them.' Edward Roper's ability to put the personal aside as an unnecessary emotional distraction is shown by the fact that shortly after this he told his poor wife to sit in a corner of the room where he could not see her, as, she told the Reverend MacCartie, 'it only made him fret when he saw me'. We are to be reminded of this extraordinary impersonality in Edward Roper when we read of Esther preparing Eva Gore-Booth for death in 1926.

God was to provide for Edward Roper's widow and children through the good offices of the Church Missionary Society. The Yoruba Mission, where Edward Roper served, was notorious for claiming the lives of all the missionaries sent there until his appointment. His success in learning Yoruba and his survival of three years' captivity had brought him to the attention of the chief officers of the Church Missionary Society. When he was imprisoned Edward Roper was sent cheering letters by Henry Venn, the Honorary Secretary of the CMS, and son of John Venn, one of the founders of the CMS in 1797, a member of the evangelising 'Clapham sect'.

Because so many of their missionaries died on service, or became ill, the welfare of widows and children was seen to very early in the Society's history. In 1850 the Church Missionary Children's Home had been founded through a Jubilee Fund that raised £55,000 'to make provision for sick and disabled missionaries and to establish a home for missionaries' children'. The note on the foundation of the home in the CMS centenary volume explains that the home was set up 'in order that the parents may apply themselves without distraction to their work as evangelists'.

From 1853–86 the home was in Highbury with an average number of eighty pupil/boarders. No allowance of any kind was made 'in respect of children living at the Church Missionary Children's Home when Resident'. What the Home boarding was worth we can calculate from the allowance given to children not at the Home. Boys and girls under ten had £10 per annum, boys from 8–15 £36 per annum, girls from 8–15 £20 per annum.

The CMS records show us exactly how Edward Roper's income changed as he progressed from lay catechist to ordained priest, then to married clergyman with children. As a lay catechist abroad he earned £50 per annum. As an ordained missionary on the continent he earned £80, with a special deputational allowance of £150 in addition to his ordinary married allowance in England of £100.

After Edward Roper's death in 1877 Annie Roper received a widow's pension of £50 per annum; she died on 29 March 1889, when Esther had been at Owens College, Manchester, for two years. Probably because of Venn's interest, the CMS saw both Esther and Reginald through their college education, but from that time on it was obviously a matter of self-support. Esther's position as suffrage union organiser was salaried, and Edward Roper, having saved, had bought a house in Manchester in 1875 which was to remain a safe base and asset for Esther and Reginald.

Annie Roper died at the age of forty-three of a fever then common in women who had had several pregnancies in a short number of years, thereby developing anaemia. Her death certificate shows that she died at home, 16 George Street, in the sub-district of Broughton in Salford, of *Anaemia Pyrexia*. Her nephew John Cummins was with her when she died. It is a curious fact that although Edward Roper had noted the careful Yoruba customs with nursing and child-bearing women, who were allowed long periods of recovery after child-bearing, he himself did not realise the importance of periods of sexual abstinence to women. He had sexual access to his wife immediately after the birth of his children. Of the four children that Annie Roper carried to full term, two were born nine months after the prevous child. Esther was a twenty year old student at Owens College when her mother died and aware enough to understand the cause of her early death.

CHAPTER 3

MANCHESTER

The industrial revolution of the eighteenth and nineteenth centuries disfigured the great cities of Northern and Midland Britain. Manchester became the industrial capital of the world and a by-word for its vulgarity and commercialism, and Mecca to that busy middle class enriching itself by commerce that the Germans came to call 'Manchestertum'. The patrician South looked down upon the brash, *arriviste* North and Midlands and was not impressed, 'Brummagem' – a slang form of Birmingham – meant cheapjack, counterfeit, sham, cheap and showy.

The conditions in which the working classes lived in these cities were appalling, and Engels, that most unlikely of Manchester mill-owners, believed that the inevitable socialist revolution would radiate from Manchester which was the natural breeding-ground for social reformers. Robert Owen – 'the Father of British Socialism' and inventor of co-operative communities – made himself a wealthy man here, but he had to move to Glasgow to put his theories into practice at New Lanark as he could not initiate reforms in Manchester.

When Engels came to Manchester in 1842 he became a supporter of the Chartist movement and of Robert Owen's theories. During two years in Manchester Engels gathered the material to write *The Conditions of the Working Class in England* and it is ironic that this study should have thrust Engels into 'Little Ireland', the slum, south-west of the Oxford Road, occupied by the Irish workers brought in as cheap labour. Engels became involved with Mary Burns, a Fenian, and they lived together until her death. The conjunction of Irish nationalism, socialism and feminism is one that we meet frequently in characters like Mrs Despard and Dr Richard Pankhurst who, knowing the state of the Irish in the lowest levels of English industrial society, interested themselves in the state of Ireland. The Irish slum was the worst in Manchester. Engels described it:

> The most horrible spot . . . . The cottages are old, dirty and of the smallest sort, the streets uneven, falling into ruts, and in parts without drains or pavements. A horde of ragged women and children swarm about here, as filthy as the swine that thrive upon the garbage heaps and in the puddles.

It was the sale of his Manchester firm in 1869 that enabled Engels to allow Marx £350 a year and for them to devote their lives to the Communist cause.

The great Manchester reformers Richard Cobden and John Bright came together in 1842 to campaign for the Repeal of the Corn Laws which had been intended to protect home-grown corn by preventing the importation of cheap foreign corn but instead caused inflation. The Corn Laws were repealed in 1846 and Bright became MP for Manchester in 1847, his name and Cobden's for ever associated with 'cheap bread for the poor'. Again we find in the Bright family, who were Quakers, the combination of pro-Irish agitation, feminism and socialism. Jacob Bright, John's brother, was one of the first MPs to put forward the women's suffrage question, and Bright's daughters became mainstays of the women's movement, notably Mrs Bright MacLaren who founded the Edinburgh Suffrage Society and who was to be a mentor of the young Esther Roper. When Mrs Cobden-Sanderson, Cobden's daughter, was imprisoned at a suffrage rally, the public outcry was immense at the insult to this daughter of the man who had given the English poor cheap bread; the involvement of the daughters of Cobden and Bright did much to give an acceptable image to the suffrage movement.

Although the Chartists did initially include suffrage for women in their demands this was dropped very early in the campaign and the People's Charter at the time Engels encountered it was a six-point charter demanding (1) manhood suffrage, (2) the ballot, (3) equal electoral districts, (4) abolition of property quali-fications, (5) payment for MPs and (6) annual parliaments.

It was not the working class that initiated the women's suffrage movement but a combination of privileged women, many from Dissenting backgrounds (it was Quaker women who initiated the

American suffrage movement), and the daughters of enlightened men like Cobden and Bright and the father of the Garrett girls: Dr Elizabeth Garrett Anderson and her sister Millicent, Mrs Henry Fawcett.

A small but vocal group, the early suffragists in many cases wished for the vote for women with a property qualification and did not see any point to the enfranchisement of working-class women. The notion that working-class women might be converted to the cause and lend 'the power of numbers' was a new one, not thought of by the early Manchester suffragists like Miss Becker. It was almost certainly the brain-child of Esther Roper.

To make the politically-alert suffragists aware of the existence of the inert mass of working-class women and vice versa was a long process. Young working girls like Selina Coombe and Sarah Reddish, unusually articulate for their time and class, became politically aware and active around 1890 but both looked initially to labour movements rather than to form any concerted woman's movement.

The upper and middle classes could close their eyes to actual conditions among the working classes but when they began to encounter the subject in their light reading they were forced to address it. In the novels of Elizabeth Gaskell we find a realistic depiction of industrial Manchester – her novel *North and South* makes a plea for reconciliation between 'masters' and 'hands' and sets out a way forward for both in co-operation. Other novels of hers like *Ruth* and *Mary Barton* give graphic detail on the lives of working-class women. A Unitarian Minister's wife, Mrs Gaskell knew her subject well: she never drove about Manchester but went everywhere on foot.

Her 'industrial' novels, like Dickens' *Hard Times*, brought to their reading public's attention the grimness of conditions suffered by such as the Manchester factory workers. Depressing as are Mrs Gaskell's descriptions it is only now with the publication of memoirs and recollections by early suffrage workers who began their working lives in the factories and mills that we can realise just what women suffered in them, and what they were accustomed to accept as their lot.

As ever, woman's sexual attributes and nature were foremost, even on the factory floor, and Selina Coombe, at work in 1891–2, remembered the sexual harassment and crudities that were common then. There was not even elementary female hygiene.

Selina, her daughter May told Jill Liddington, was almost sacked for helping a fellow worker to make sanitary towels out of cotton waste:

> Women in those days didn't wear any sanitary protection; all their petticoats would be covered in blood every month . . . anyhow this girl's mother came back and played pop at the mill with the manager, because my mother had given this girl some towels. She said how was her daughter ever going to get off if they didn't know about this smell? Like an animal! My mother said there used to be blood on the floor of the winding room . . . it went straight down onto the floor, or on to the petticoats. It was an attraction . . .

Selina objected to the working girls' mute acceptance of male sexual reverence as bleeding sacred cows. Deep feelings of self-loathing and lack of confidence, even, that one rated as human rather than bestial seemed to Selina to make women dumb. Obviously the women who first walked into these factory precincts as suffrage organisers were extraordinarily courageous and patient. When Eva and Esther began living together it was noticeable that Eva, working apart from Esther with Sarah Dickenson, concentrated on the Labour Union where she lectured on poetry and plays and tried to wake young factory women from their stultified lives. She concentrated more on the personal, it was her especial gift, where Esther campaigned at the factories with pamphlets and speeches, her aide was the stalwart Sarah Reddish, four-square and hatless. Hats, to such as Sarah, were bourgeois symbols of male oppression. Over-decorated, cumbersome objects designed to conceal the 'distracting glory' of a woman's hair, hats were scorned by radical women.

With such an attitude to menstruation prevalent in the factories and mills, total ignorance of efficient contraception was common and repeated child-bearing was the chief cause of ill health amongst women. Those women who were brave enough to tackle the problem openly and in print, like Mrs Wolstenholme Elmy, actually put forward as a 'safe period' that time when, we know now, a woman was most likely to conceive.

Mrs Wolstenholme Elmy had been in the forefront of the Manchester suffrage society since its foundation in 1865, campaigning for higher education for women, suffrage and reform of the marriage laws, but her views on sexuality were most unconventional and brave. She promoted what she called 'psychic love' between the sexes and did not think that sexual intercourse was necessary except for reproduction. She asked for sexual self-control from men in order that women could avoid 'the degradation of her temple to solely animal uses'. Esther, familiar with Wolstenholme Elmy, would have gained confidence from Elmy's assurance that women need not feel the compulsion to marry – that it was acceptable to choose to stay unmarried – not a social disgrace. In her book *Woman Free* Mrs Elmy, in a poem intended as a sex-education aid, wrote:

> For but a slave man must ever be,
> Till she to shape her own career be free; –
> Free from all uninvited touch of man,
> Free mistress of her person's sacred plan . . .

Unusual ideas on sexuality also reached Esther through Enid Stacy, her friend and co-worker from 1895, who worked with Edward Carpenter. Stacy contributed *A Century of Women's Rights* to Carpenter's anthology of socialist writing *Forecasts of the Coming Century* published by the Manchester Labour Press in 1897.

Carpenter's views on marriage were revolutionary, he published his *Love's Coming of Age* (also with the Manchester Labour Press) in 1896. His views on love between persons of the same sex he published widely, naming the affection 'homogenic love' rather than homosexual. Some of his ideas are echoed, years later, in the magazine *Urania*, with which Esther and Eva were connected for many years. For whatever reasons, in their mid-twenties Esther and Eva were perfectly contented to be unmarried and to work for and with women.

But Eva could not have chosen a place more ruinous to her constitution than Manchester. Supposedly suffering from consumption Eva came to a city described by Mrs Gaskell:

> For several miles before they reached M—, they saw a deep, lead coloured cloud hanging over the horizon in the direction in which it lay. It was all the darker from contrast with the pale grey blue of the wintry sky; for in Heston there had been the

earliest sign of frost. Nearer to the town, the air had a faint
taste and smell of smoke . . .

Happy as Eva was to live and work with Esther, her first years in
Manchester inspired her to write poetry yearning for the sight of
home. As an aristocratic woman, Eva Gore-Booth was not made
aware of the difficulties in the way of ordinary women who
wished for an education. Esther Roper was indeed fortunate in
this respect that her home town was Manchester.

In her college education Esther presents a complete contrast to
her partner who was tutored one-to-one by a much-loved
governess on the lawns or in the schoolroom of Lissadell. Esther
was amongst the very first batch of women to present themselves
for degrees at Victoria University, Manchester. Although the
revolution in women's education had begun mid-century in
London with the establishment of Queens (1848) and Bedford
(1849) Colleges, in Manchester in the 1880s the process of
introducing women into the sacred groves of academe as serious
degree students rather than ticket-holding sight-seers was painfully slow and fraught with bogeys that are hardly imaginable to
women of the 1980s.

The main stumbling-block in the 1880s to the education of
women was the difficulty, on the part of men, in accepting that
women were distinct human beings capable of living independ-
ently of men. When John Owens founded his Manchester college
'for instructing and improving young persons of the male sex' in
1851 there was, naturally, no thought of provision for women,
and over the next thirty years the supporters of women's education, including some distinguished men within Owens College,
worked their tortuous way to subvert the provisions of Owens'
will to provide for the 'male sex' only.

The three major obstacles before women wishing for higher
education in Manchester were – first, the legal prohibition in
Owens' will, second, looming large, the then-defective condition
of women's education and, last, very strong public opinion
against the higher education of women 'especially if it was given
to men and women in the same classrooms'! In brief: higher
education for women at Owens would be illegal, unnecessary and
would lead to immorality.

Always depending upon the broad-mindedness of their
menfolk, it was often possible for women in the English upper

classes to get themselves an education if they wished to. An answering broad-mindedness in the men of the middle classes was asked for after the industrial revolution when large numbers of the English middle class became very wealthy and powerful but did not alter in a primitive attitude to the education of girl children: it was actually believed to be harmful to their prospects in life.

In the Manchester area the question of educating girls at last became a live issue, widely reported in the press, and much debated in public, with the publication of the Schools Enquiry Commission of 1864. Mark Pattison, Chief Commissioner, was reduced to cold criticism: 'An average man of the middle classes prefers a woman who is less educated to one who is more. The preference of a man for a less cultivated woman arises from his own want of culture. Culture has not kept pace with wealth . . . .' He summed up the defects of women's education in a crushing tally: 'Want of thoroughness and foundation, want of system, slovenliness and showy superficiality, inattention to rudiments, undue time given to accomplishments and these not taught intelligently or in any scientific manner' and, the last, 'want of organisation'. Part of the Schools Enquiry Report had a bearing on Manchester – the citadel of English industrial wealth – and a bastion of male prejudice to the education of women.

James Bryce, who was responsible for the Lancashire section of the Report, was especially caustic at the lack of endowments for the secondary education of girls. In the whole of England there were 572 endowed secondary schools for boys with an attendance of 36,000 and only fourteen for girls with an attendance of 1,100. Not one of these fourteen endowed schools for girls was in Lancashire. Bryce commented: 'the two capital defects of the teachers of girls are these: they have not themselves been well taught and they do not know how to teach'. He thundered on: 'the notion that women had minds as cultivable and as well worth cultivating as men's minds is still regarded by the ordinary British parent as an offensive, not to say revolutionary paradox'.

In Manchester open battle was engaged and in 1870 a new college was incorporated under the name of 'Owens Extension College'. West of the Oxford Road were the old college buildings where the men were taught, to the east in Brunswick Street was founded a house for the first women students where they were lectured in selected subjects by lecturers from 'across the road'.

Now the cat was in sight of the pigeons. The splendid tactics of the women's champions were to isolate Owens in public opinion, plant a separate (but associated) institution on its boundary, and invade by osmosis.

Bridling against this questionable woman-thing now alongside them, be she ever so lightweight and amateur, the Principal of Owens College formed and headed a conservative group opposed to women studying with men. This group of conservative academics evidently thought that the earnest young ladies of Brunswick Street, many of them bespectacled, were bent on the seduction of innocent young males within the classroom. In April 1875 the *Manchester Examiner* published a letter asking for the opening of classes to women in Owens and ridiculing the chief objection of the Principal's diehards: 'arrangements could be made for securing the effective separation of students of different sexes when attending lectures for the purposes of instruction'. The thought of sexual activity, perhaps at floor level in the Lecture Room, obviously fired the imaginations of the alarmists. A series of letters pro and con flew back and forth with the male correspondent, who rather predictably signed himself 'Governor', flatly concluding 'the admission of women would be unfair to those who wished to use the College as a place of quiet study'.

Nothing daunted, the women's party founded in 1877 a Manchester and Salford College for Women. It was not directly connected with Owens, but they did 'associate'. The building was a gloomy house near the main Owens buildings. In 1880, a final step – a new charter for the Victoria University, Manchester, a federation of separate Colleges – recognised the equality of women students, but Owens still refused them entry.

A further barrage of letters in the press quoted testimony from Henry Morley and Stanley Jevons of University College, London, to the 'good effects of the presence of women in the classes', and much other evidence was presented to show that 'men and women could work together without evil results'. When Esther Roper entered Victoria University, Manchester, in October 1886, the evil muddle in the minds of Owens' governors was still in full sway; her academic status as a woman was not in the least clear, she was not at that stage an accredited student. It was not until 1891 that she took her degree, a second division in History, because it was only in 1888 that the Council of Owens College was empowered to admit women to any class higher than matriculation grade and that scholarships were thrown open. There remained one last bastion which was revealed when the women claimed the right to practise medicine. Professor Fiddes, in his introduction to *The History of Women at Manchester University*, commented that:

> It was as though an attacking army had begun by hurling itself on the enemy where he was most strongly entrenched, for a great body of respectable opinion was genuinely revolted by the idea that women be allowed to study the human body.

And, not surprisingly, it is among the medical professors and students that we find the strongest antagonism to women appearing amongst them in their sacred enclosure of learning in Manchester.

Conservative male opinion was irritatedly conscious of the first 'New Women' in the University, Esther Roper among them. Her type was candidly, and publicly, abhorred by the medics. From 1895 there are references to *New Women* in the Owens College Magazine, uncomplimentary ones, and we find the fact that in 1895 at the Medical Dinner of that year the *New Woman* was excluded, by special announcement when the toast 'To the Ladies' was given. Clearly university life for women in Manchester in the 1880s and 1890s was formative, and bitterly so, for those like Esther who were concerned with the emancipation of women. Reformation of character as women begins with them for they were the first to be seen as capable of sitting for degrees – to be examined by men – and to be found 'not wanting'. In 1883 there were eighty girls attending the College for Women but very few of these presented themselves for examination. Miss Amy Bulley (a graduate of Newnham, founded 1871), secretary to the College, tried hard to make the girls sit examinations but they had 'a horror of being examined'. The college had been in operation for six years by 1883, and, very cautiously, Owens agreed to accept *some* women into *some* classes for a trial period of five years. Dr Mabel Tylecote, the author of *The Education of Women at Manchester University*, in describing this momentous event shows how Principal Greenwood, whom she described as 'a somewhat nervous reformer', masterminded a system whereby a 'separate but annexed' institution should provide for women with admission to 'some' classes in Owens. Dr Tylecote gives, with relish, a popular student joke of the time about the College Arms. These showed a snake rearing to the sun; the motto is *Arduus ad Solem*. The sun is like a face looking over a battlement and this, student wits maintained, represented Principal Greenwood 'watching the advance of the snake woman across the Oxford Road'.

Edith Wilson, sister of Archdeacon J. M. Wilson, was appointed by the College as Assistant Secretary and Tutor in the Department of Women at a salary of £100 p.a. and it was she who took Esther Roper under her wing when Esther, a serious schoolgirl fresh from her CMS Boarding School in London, became a Manchester University student. Very few of the women were brave enough to study for degrees at this time – on average, of 68 students only 16 attempted degrees. Half of the female students were 'Ladies' – unregistered students who carried cards admitting them to single courses of lectures; these were distinct from the 'women' who were registered, full-time students.

Esther's mother had been bold and unconventional in allowing her to be one of these 'women' and study for a degree. At the request of the college authorities she had written a letter assuring them that Esther's 'course of study may be entered on without the prospect of injury to her health'. The authorities remained anxious over the suitability of women for brain work and as late as 1903 women students were required to provide such a letter from their parent or guardian certifying them fit for such work.

Traditional medical opinion held that education was bad for women's health. It was 'unfortunate as well as sad', as Dr Mabel wrote, that one of the first degree students, Annie Eastwood, died of tuberculosis before completing her degree course. Her doctor, Dr John Thorburn, Professor of Obstetrics at Manchester, publicised his opinion that there was a direct connection between tuberculosis and the 'over-education' of women. He published a letter in which he argued that 'women were incapable of following an unbroken routine of work, and of accepting the fixed times of examinations without permanent injury to their health'. He claimed that for women a degree course was 'one of the dangerous occupations of life' and maintained that one session of 'undue mental strain' could end a career – 'No physician will deny this for a moment.' It was hardly helpful or fair on the first women students at Owens to be so publicly slighted but fortunately Thorburn was succeeded by a (rare) pro-woman medic, Dr

Collingworth, and his women students took care to undo Thorburn's damage to their cause by maintaining that 'women suffered more harm from having nothing to do than they ever did from over-work'.

Despite this reform within the department of obstetrics itself, the medic at large in Owens remained a monster of conservative bigotry. The Owens College Magazine prints a poem by jolly Dr Bradley who regaled the guests at another Medical Dinner with his poem:

> As nurses nice you look I gladly own
> but, armed with scalpel, woman I disown.
> Th' encircling arm, which guides you the right way
> In life's quick waltz should be your tourniquet.

In spite of diehard opposition, that had its core in the Medical Department, when in 1886 the 'experiment' of educating women in Owens was reviewed, it was deemed a success, and pro-women academics like Professor Ward and Professor Tout (Ward and Tout were both Esther's professors) had much to do with this gradual conversion of opinion. But when we read, in the College Magazine or in Dr Tylecote's account, of the actual physical intrusion of women into Owens the process was laughably stealthy and protracted.

The headquarters of the Women's Department was the old house in Brunswick Street (numbers 223–5) until 1897. 'Even those who cherish an affection for this building recall it as gloomy and dingy, full of draughts and smoking chimneys.' It was only 'degree girls' like Esther who went across to Owens to attend senior classes. Miss Wilson had to chaperone any solitary woman. The first woman to attend classes in College, brave girl, on wet days had to prop her umbrella beside her; she 'caused first a pool and then a stream which absorbed the pleased attention of the class'. So that it came to pass that the first property owned by the women in Owens College was 'the famous umbrella stand acquired in 1886'. From this small beginning came a gradual improvement of the women's lot in the College. They were given a Common Room – 'a little room under the roof, approached by a small staircase behind an iron gate'. It was entered through the back-quarters of the Museum, through a corridor which was a repository for mouldy and unregarded stuffed wild animals including a gorilla and a lion. Principal Greenwood continued to shine as a neurotic calamity-monger. When he granted the use of a room near the Owens Library to a girls' high school teacher who wished to read there he delicately 'drew her attention to the fact that she could lock herself in'.

Further progress in acquiring territory was made in 1888 when Dr Ward, the Professor of History, saw Edith Johnstone (Classical Honours) filling the kettle for tea at a tap on the middle corridor. Mary Johnstone (First Class Honours, History), her sister, described what happened next:

> Bending from his stately height, he filled it for her and bore it up to the eyrie in the roof, saw how small the room was, and talked with the Principal, who at once kindly offered the women a small Common Room at the end of the second corridor, and two dressing rooms above it.

This brought a great improvement in facilities – up in the eyrie the teacups had been washed in firebuckets.

So Esther's group of women students slowly came out into the open. It took some time for the men students to react and comment. Women are not mentioned in the Owens College Magazine until 1891–2. Out of 141 pages precisely two columns, one page in all, give information from the Department for Women. 'Types of College Men', a seven-part series I–VII, takes up sixteen pages. Then, in October of 1892, there is a blinding flash of light and revelation: pages 24–5, 'Types of College Men – and Women. No. VIII':

VIII. The Lady Student
Following the fashion which has come into vogue in the last few years, we at Owens are favoured with the presence of a certain number of lady students .... Rumour speaks of a terribly severe code of rules which lady students have to subscribe to before entering the College, and the fact of its existence is favoured by the conduct and behaviour of the ladies themselves, for they hold themselves entirely aloof from their fellow students of the male persuasion, never speaking to nor holding any communication with them, even keeping them at a distance in the class room, where they appropriate a particular row of seats, upon which they expect no man ever to

trespass . . . . The Lady Students do not join any of the Union Societies, and such subjects as Women's Suffrage and Education are discussed at the Debating Society without the ladies having any say in the matter . . . . But Mrs Grundy still reigns supreme at Owens, notwithstanding the new idea of this *fin de siècle* age, and until she is dethroned from her power, we cannot hope for that freedom of intercourse between all classes of students at Owens – men and women alike – from which both would derive an equal benefit.

This was written by a student, J. H. Bailey, in 1892 just after Esther's graduation, and it was a very gradual process through the nineties that opened up debates to the women and revolutionised the social life of the college. In the years during which Esther was a student the women deliberately kept a very low profile indeed in order to avoid what was called 'sex antagonism' and also to avoid any possible accusations of that immorality hinted at by the alarmists in the mid-eighties. They avoided confrontation with men wherever possible, as Bailey's article on 'College Women' shows, and when the women set up their own Debating Society they avoided mentioning 'Women' in the society's title; it was demurely christened the Social Debating Society. The SDS at the beginning was attended by 10–20 members and it was at these women-only debates that Esther found her feet as a public speaker. She often chaired SDS meetings.

On 7 March 1893, numbers of early women graduates, including an impressive array of firsts, were admitted to the Council of Owens College as Associates, Esther being among them. This did give the women a new-found confidence. As a graduate Associate, Esther was an officer of the SDS and other women's societies throughout the 1890s although her paid jobs with the National Society for Women's Suffrage began in 1894. The College Magazine in its 'News of the Women's Department' column congratulates her in October 1894 and comments: 'Many readers of this Magazine will probably already have heard that Miss Roper, B.A., a student of this College, has been appointed a Secretary of the National Society for Women's Suffrage.' In this year Esther put the motion 'that Women should have equal rights with Men' and only carried the motion by the casting vote of the President, Miss Wilson, Esther's old mentor. When the SDS debated the entry of women into Parliament, the motion was carried, but again only by one vote. After Esther's introduction of the subject, the suffrage question gained ground in debating circles, and it became a popular topic with the men. For example, on 29 February 1897 the Law Students Society and Owens College Union (OCU) Debating Society debated the motion that 'the Parliamentary Franchise should be extended to women'. It was debated hotly for three hours, the resolution being lost by a majority of seven.

In the spring of 1885 a student, H. Roxburghe, published an article On 'the New Woman' in the College Magazine, giving a most revealing catalogue of stereotypes.

> She smokes. She rides a bicycle – not in skirts. She demands a vote. She belongs to a club. She would like a latch key, if she has not already got one. She holds drawing room meetings, and crowds to public halls to discuss her place in the world. (I am informed that a deaf chairwoman is usually elected, so that she may assent to the business of the meeting, untroubled by the disgraceful nature of the proceedings. I have also been informed by a credible witness that at one such meeting the lady in the chair concluded her remarks with the statement that after long and serious thought, she had come to one important conclusion that women ought not to wear bonnets in church) . . . . She is no longer content to exert the sweet influence of her sex, but stakes her hopes upon power. She is therefore odious . . . (but) . . . is this extravagantly noisy person of today really more objectionable or more hurtful to the community than was her silly forerunner [he cites the women of Dickens and Thackeray as examples] of a hundred years ago?
>
> The conditions of woman's life are new, and she must develop where she is allowed to breathe . . . [he concludes, with a hope] that we shall escape the supreme danger of reckoning as a virtue a miserable artificial passivity which deadens the finest instincts of womanhood.

Clearly Esther's cause won friends among the Owens' men. The ground was well and truly prepared for the visit by Mrs Fawcett to Owens. On 13 February she spoke for the SDS in the History Theatre on 'Women's Suffrage', a meeting that was open to the public. A capacity audience voted on the motion 'that it is desirable to extend the Parliamentary Franchise to duly qualified women'. Progress had been made in the years since Esther first put this motion – no women, and only two men, now opposed it.

Mrs Fawcett, opening the debate, had delivered an incisive speech. She tore straight into an attack on the unrepresentative nature of the government of the day which she described as despotic:

> Few of you present will not have given some thought to the principles upon which representative government is based. The superior attraction of a benevolent despotism is an untenable position ... the rights and interests of any and every person are only secured from being disregarded when the person is able and habitually disposed to stand up for them; and secondly, the type of character and the idea of private and public duty evolved in a self-governing community are far higher than in one where the people have nothing to do with the laws but to obey them, and nothing to do with the taxes but to pay them.

The picture of Mrs Fawcett as the leader and epitome of a softly-spoken, staid and 'wet' type of woman, given credence by the Women's Social and Political Union (WSPU) wits and critics, is hardly borne out by the long report of her speech given in the Owens College Magazine. She boldly attacked the current laws on illegitimacy:

> God gives to every child two parents, the law only recognises one; where the child is born in honour and prosperity that one is the father, but where the child is born in dishonour and misery that one is the mother .... It seems as if the term 'man' in an Act of Parliament only includes women where there is anything to pay or some penalty to suffer. Where there is anything to get, it is for the man only; where there is anything to pay, the woman was graciously allowed to have the privilege.

It is pleasant to picture Mrs Fawcett thus briskly denouncing the law whilst dressed in the splendid robes of a Doctor of Laws, an honour recently conferred on her by St Andrews University. Her speech was punctuated by enthusiastic applause. She was given a reception afterwards in the Old Library where were all the distinguished ladies of Manchester including Esther, Mrs Swanwick, Mrs Tout, Mrs Pilkington Turner, Miss Potts, and many others.

By the turn of the century Esther was a woman of some prominence in Manchester through her work with the University Settlement, the Suffrage Societies and as an officer in the Women's Department of the University. In December of 1901 at a general meeting of the Associaties of Owens College Esther's name was put forward as the candidate to be first woman Governor of the College by Mrs Alfred Haworth (first Secretary of the Women's Union) and Miss Alice Crompton (First in Classics 1889): 'they felt that the 200 women students and 90 women Associates had needs and interests which required representation' but Dr William Thorburn beat Esther by two votes.

By this stage Owens' men were in general agreement that their women students, staff and Associates were a good thing; they certainly revolutionised social life. Parties, musical evenings, dances and theatricals thrived. Some of the Senior Members of the University took great delight in attending the dances in the Women's Union arranged by the Cinderella Club. This had been founded by Dr Marie Stopes, later champion of contraception, then a member of the teaching staff in the Botany Department. The Women's Union, the Women's Athletic Union and Ashburne House, the first women's Hall of Residence, had all been founded in 1899. With the popularity of the Women's Union 'socials' came a spate of joint societies, the earliest being the photographic, philosophic and historical societies, quickly followed by the classical and biological. By about 1906 it was usual for these joint societies to have both a man and a woman secretary, and mixed committees. The integration of the two sexes within Owens perhaps helps to explain why the women at the outbreak of the First World War almost as one took the Pankhurst line – supported 'their men' and aided the war effort. Pacifism was not mentioned, a fact that further explains Eva and Esther's lack of repute for they were, they admitted, 'extreme pacifists'.

The Education of Women at Manchester University mentions Esther fleetingly twice, even the bare facts of her work for the NUWSS, the Women's Peace Crusade, Conscientious Objectors, and the Women's International League for Peace and Freedom (WILPF) rate no mention. There is a single reference to pacifism in the entire book, in the chapter, 'War 1914–1918':

It is worthy of record that in 1916 Miss Maude Royden, perhaps the most outstanding woman pacifist, was a guest of honour at the Women's Union. She referred to her pacifist faith and sought to express herself in such a way as to minimise the embarrassment which her presence at the time occasioned to some of her hostesses.

Manchester's detestation of pacifism surfaced when it was offered, as a picture donation to the Manchester Art Gallery, a portrait of Margaret Ashton, one of the city's most distinguished daughters. Margaret Ashton gave her entire working life to the causes of women's suffrage and peace, she was chairman of the NESWS in 1906 and helped to found the WILPF in 1915. Manchester Art Gallery refused the gift of her portrait, by Henry Lamb, because of her 'pacifist opinions'.

CHAPTER 4

EVA GORE-BOOTH BECOMES A SUFFRAGIST

Eva returned to Lissadell from Italy in the autumn of 1896 full of women's suffrage. Constance was instantly infected and at a meeting at Breaghway Old School, Constance was elected President, Eva secretary and Mabel treasurer of the Sligo branch of the Irish Women's Suffrage and Local Government Association. Esther Roper's indoctrination of Eva during her holiday had been intense and thorough. *The Sligo Champion* of 26 December 1896 gives us a record of the speeches of the Gore-Booth sisters at a public meeting at the Milltown National School in Drumcliffe on behalf of women's suffrage. It was patronisingly given the headline 'Amusing Proceedings'.

Constance, presiding, exhorted the women present to speak out on their own behalf as she recalled the argument that women were not given the suffrage because 'they did not demand it with sufficient force and noise'. She rallied them with 'Silence is an evil that might easily be remedied, and the sooner we begin to make a row the better.'

Constance presided over this meeting with great brio, managing hecklers with ease, but was as lightly engaged with the cause as with a theatrical part. It was quite other with Eva who spoke here in public for the first time on behalf of the cause to which she was to remain true throughout her life. She spoke of co-operation: 'I should like to call on Irishwomen to follow the example of the farmers of Drumcliffe, and to insist, in spite of opposition, in taking their affairs into their own hands,' and of community: 'All of us, men and women alike, besides our immediate duties to our families, have duties to our neighbours, and to our country, and to society at large. Charity begins at home, but it should not end there.'

For numbers of men and women like Eva who came to realise the rottenness of lower levels of British society through the work of men like William Booth, Mayhew, Toynbee and W. T. Stead, feelings of guilt, rejection of their own class and the crying need for reparation led them to leave their homes and families and throw in their lot with Settlement communities to live amongst the poor. At this time, and in this situation, 'charity' was a loaded word.

Arnold Toynbee, the young Oxford historian who pioneered slum work in London's East End, said that the wealthy had sinned in 'offering charity and not justice' to the poor. When Toynbee died in 1883 his friends founded Toynbee Hall as a memorial to him and it was this institution that served as a model for the Manchester University Settlement in the slums of Ancoats where Eva first worked when she joined Esther in Manchester.

On 27 March 1895, a meeting was held at the Union in Owens College to discuss the setting up of a University Settlement. Canon Barrett (Warden of Toynbee Hall) came to address the meeting; it had been organised by Dr Ward. Canon Barrett explained what a Settlement was:

> Simply a club of University men and women established in some industrial centre. A party of men and women in touch with educated opinion took a house and made their lives in neighbourhoods occupied chiefly by working people . . . . They associated together for purpose of entertainment, consultation and practical duty . . . they got to know how the majority of their fellow-citizens really lived. They got to know what it meant to live in a narrow street in a smoke-laden atmosphere with dull and mean sights around them; what it meant to live in a neighbourhood where there were no playgrounds, no open spaces.

Canon Barrett reminded his audience of Disraeli's warnings that England would become two nations of the poor and of the rich and he felt that Settlements could do something to abate that growing antagonism. Mr Pilkington Turner then moved a resolution to establish 'an organisation of social work'; speaking on behalf of the group of graduates who were to open the Settlement:

> They felt that it would be a disgrace if those who had so many privileges and opportunities . . . did not do more than they had done in the past to use their lives in a wise and generous way. In all they did they sought to act in a spirit of humility and sympathy, and without such a spirit it were better not to act . . .

On 17 May an Executive Committee was formed. Esther and Miss Wilson would have no tokenism and they objected to preferential treatment for women candidates for the Executive when Mr Smythe 'gallantly' moved that six of each sex be elected, and the names of those chosen be the first six in order of nomination. Miss Wilson and Miss Roper, although appreciating the compliment to the women contained in the resolution, thought it would be taking unfair advantage, and preferred to meet the men on equal terms. They therefore moved and seconded respectively, as an amendment, 'That the choice be left to the meeting', which was carried. The election, which then took place amid intense excitement, certainly justified the amendment, as all the women candidates were elected. These were Miss (Dr) Anderson, Miss Cooke, Miss Lang, Miss Roper, Miss Southern, and Miss Stoehr.

When we read accounts of the 'entertainment and education' programme undertaken by the Settlement from its headquarters in Ancoats Hall, Canon Barrett's lightness of description becomes apparent, for the programme involved long exhausting hours of work. Alice Crompton, the women's Warden, describes one winter season of six months 1898–9. Twelve educational classes had been running. There were seventy-three free entertainments – lectures, concerts and children's evenings. A Little Girls' Club was open three nights a week, the Settlement Lads' Club in the Jersey Street Dwellings was open every night. There were numerous 'At Homes' at Ancoats Hall. Twice large parties were taken to the theatre, eighty went to see Benson in *Twelfth Night* and ninety to see the *Winter's Tale*. The Wednesday Evening Concerts had attendances of around 400.

This was a large institution; its work was reviewed after five years in the Owens College Union Magazine in 1900 when Dr Ward, the man who was largely responsible for the founding of the Settlement, moved on after his election as Master of Peterhouse in Cambridge. The writer urges more undergraduates to give time to the Settlement:

A walk of twenty minutes from College brings one to the foot of Every Street, where stands the fine old house known as the Art Museum or Ancoats Hall. Here activities of a very varied nature are being carried out. One room may contain an audience of twenty-five to eighty in number listening to a popular lecture with lantern slides, to a practical discourse on Local Government, to one more erudite on Psychology or Evolution. In a larger room are assembled about seventy folk of all ages and upbringings playing games, chatting, hearing or giving songs and recitations, learning to know and sympathise with one another. Upstairs some dozen men, under the leadership of a resident, are practising the instrumental parts of an operetta to be produced by the choral society. At the end of the corridor fourteen artisans and clerks are 'treading the primrose paths' of botanical lore, under the guidance of a newly-graduated Owens man. Relegated to the attic a band of work girls are rehearsing Macbeth . . .

Preparing the work girls for their Shakespearean performance was Eva. One of the work girls, Louisa Smith who became a lifelong friend, wrote to Esther of Eva's class:

We were a class of about sixteen girls. I think we were all machinists and we *were* rough . . . . We called ourselves the Elizabethan Society because we had no scenery: as we said among ourselves, we had no assets, but we enjoyed every minute of the rehearsals. We were very raw material but keen on acting; she showed such patience and love that we would do anything to please her and she got the best out of us. After rehearsals we would give a show of our own, an imitation of what we had seen or imagined . . . . If any of us were feeling seedy or worried about business or home she could always see, and showed such an understanding sympathy that we came away feeling we had a real friend . . . . We thought she was a being from another world. I don't think I exaggerate when I say we worshipped her, but she never knew it, she was so utterly selfless . . .

Eva had a fore-runner in philanthropic work in Manchester in her great uncle Henry. It was common for the gentry to keep church livings in the family should any sons go in for the church. Sir Henry Gore-Booth, who had the gift of the living, appointed his uncle, the Reverend Henry Francis Gore-Booth, to be the Rector of Sacred Trinity, Salford, in 1885. A mercantile fortune made by an early Booth had been put to good use in a charitable trust; and the same Humphrey Booth, merchant of Salford, had founded Sacred Trinity Church in 1635. He had founded the charity five years before, in 1630, and it was named, after him, the Booth Trust. He must have been a most successful merchant as by 1899 the income of the Booth Trust was £16,000 a year.

There were over 7,000 poor in the parish of Sacred Trinity, and the Reverend Henry Gore-Booth worked amongst them with the assistance of three curates and two of the Horbury Sisters, from an Anglican order of nuns, as well as many voluntary helpers. He was on the Board of the Salford School, and a member of the Committee of the Industrial Schools, of which Eva eventually became a member. He died unmarried on 4 October 1903, so that Eva had his example before her for the first six years of her residence in Manchester, and this impressive man must have been a major inspiration to her.

Eva found Settlement work absorbing and rewarding and her band of co-workers a self-sufficient co-operative community. Settlement workers had a special aura. Described by sarcastic and doubting people as the 'Toynbee cranks' they appeared very different to the young Teresa Billington Greig whose first escape from an unpleasant family life came with her discovery of the Settlement.

Teresa Billington Greig thought of the family circle as being 'chained' for all time to people with whom one might have nothing in common and even positively dislike; she suffered an over-religious Catholic upbringing and was a witness to the miserable broken-down marriage of her parents. Troubled and unhappy, she attended an event at Ancoats Hall and met Settlement workers: 'I liked their faces. They were quiet and attentive faces, kindly and responsive, neither smug nor superior nor sanctimonious, not actually welcoming but accepting in kindness you and and whatever you brought to them . . .'

Up until her visit to the Settlement, Teresa had been unable to associate true good intention with any of the social work she had seen and experienced in Manchester. She was highly critical of the self-satisfaction and radiant smugness of the religious do-gooders of the benevolent institutions sponsored by the many church sects in the city. In her autobiography, in note form, she writes of the 'Settlement Period' as of seminal importance to her:

> This should have a 'pleasant awakening' section of its own – the atmosphere – the contact with responsive people – with warmth – with enquiring minds – social service a basic idea – without the mawkish attitude met in religious circles – a sound healthy practical outlook prevailed – nobody preached or prayed at you . . . . There was no fuss, no scared avoidance of difference and no sense of dominance. Ancoats Hall, Carr Meadow and the Round House had the atmosphere of toler- ance – that tolerant acceptance of all who were members and of their opinions which should be the essence of the home – and because of the sense of property-relationship in the family is so utterly absent there . . .

At Ancoats Hall there was a very lively debating society, much loved and well attended, called the Toynbee Debating Society. The debates there were so fast and furious that Miss Crompton noticed that the women were too terrified to stand and speak, so she founded one for women, for them to get practice and confidence, and named it after Mrs Fawcett. At 'the Fawcett' Teresa learned to use her very great skill as a public speaker, a wonderful gift to the Pankhursts' WSPU in later years, and here she came across Esther and Eva. As Teresa discovered, the Settlement absorbed people with a very wide range of the most unorthodox views. She herself was on the road to agnosticism when she first started speaking at the Fawcett. Dissatisfaction with established religion and the insti- tution of the family led many like her to take up freethinking. In Eva's case, when she first came to Manchester she had not yet discovered theosophy or seriously studied Eastern mysticism, and we find her – on her move to England – attracted to the beliefs of the more eccentric ministers of the Unitarian sect.

Unitarianism had always attracted freethinkers like Coleridge who practised as a Unitarian minister for a time; their doctrines rejected the miraculous conception, the ascension into heaven, and the worship of Christ as divine. They believed him to be a man 'with no other power than can properly be assigned to a human being'. As a popular joke had it: 'They believe in at MOST one God.' The Church was well established in Manchester and prominent amongst its ministers were the Rev. William Gaskell – husband of Mrs Gaskell, the novelist – who was minister at Cross Street Unitarian Chapel, and his successor there, the Rev. Steinthal, who was involved with the women's suffrage cause in Manchester from the very beginning and who was a staunch supporter of Eva and Esther throughout their careers. But the most remarkable Unitarian minister to influence them was John Trevor, minister of Upper Brook Street Free Church, 1890–1, who founded the Labour Church in 1891. Both Eva and Esther gave talks and lectures for this Church in the late nineties. From John Trevor's description of his founding of the Labour Church in its journal *The Labour Prophet* (motto: 'Let Labour be the basis of civil society' – Mazzini) we can see why this Church in particular attracted them.

Like Teresa Billington Greig finding responsiveness and her 'pleasant awakening' at the Settlement, John Trevor, in his first year of ministry in Manchester, felt that he had come into a circle of true friends:

From being quite a lonely thinker, I became a half-despairing preacher in the wilderness; and then, from being a preacher in the wilderness, I suddenly found myself in the midst of a large and goodly company, trusted and befriended as I had never dared to hope to be . . .

This was one minister who did not encourage his congregation to suffer their earthly troubles in silence and think on their future reward in heaven. He was with them in the here and now, right down to earth, and soon had a large following. On his very first Sunday in Manchester he preached in the morning on 'The Voice of Nature' and in the evening on 'The Final Report on the Sweating System'. He wrote of this time:

I wanted to get the people outside the walls of their church . . . into vital relations with the Living God and the Outcast Poor

. . . the more I realised the vastness of the problem to be solved, the more impatient did I become to get out in the open, and to take the church with me. I wanted it to be the centre of a new religious and special life in Manchester . . .

Conversations with working men, who freely admitted their great personal liking for Trevor, taught him that many working men did not enter the church, being repelled by the atmosphere; it was not one 'in which a working man could breathe freely'.

He realised 'that if working men were to have a church they must have one of their own up-building, and no other church could possibly help them . . .' John Trevor organised his Labour Church to coincide with the founding of a true 'Labour' party, as it was becoming painfully clear that Liberal and Conservative candidates simply did not have the interest of the working class at heart. Trevor had been profoundly influenced by an address by a colleague, Philip Wicksteed, at the London National Triennial Conference of Unitarian Churches in April 1891, and in this address we find described the principle which led Eva and Esther to give their working life to the University Settlement, the Lancashire and Cheshire Women's Textiles and Other Workers Representation Committee, the Trades Council, and the Labour Church.

If I say that all questions of industrial organisation are to be regarded simply and without qualification from the point of view of the worker, that the employer, the professional man, the artist, the statesman, the man of science, the poet – all who do not in the strictest sense 'make' their living – must stand or fall by the simple test of whether they make life more truly worth living to the hewers of wood and drawers of water; if I say that culture, and beauty and knowledge are pagan and inhuman, so long as they are the privilege of a caste and are built upon the toil of a subject race excluded from their enjoyment, I may be denounced as a revolutionist, but I am simply stating the very root principle of Christianity . . . . We have long talked of Brotherhood but we have never yet realised the deep meaning of it. Man has been the slave and the tool of man, and we have not understood how unbrotherly such bondage was . . .

These are ideas that will be echoed by Edward Carpenter later, and that Eva and Esther transferred to the world of women.

1 Lissadell, County Sligo, from the air.

Eva Gore Booth

Hold · the · hye · wey · and · lat · thy · gost · thee · lede ·

2 Eva Gore-Booth's bookplate. She designed this in her late teens, using a quotation from Geoffrey Chaucer's *Balade de bon conseyl*. Skeat's 1923 edition gives the full exhortation:

Forth, pilgrim, forth!
Forth, beste, out of thy stal!
Know thy contree, look up, thank God of al;
Hold the hye wey, and lat thy gost thee lede:
And trouthe shal delivere, hit is no drede.
(XIII, *Truth*, p. 122)

'Gost' has the meaning here of spirit or soul, so that Eva showed very early in life her strong bent for mysticism. In her suffrage work she wanted, literally, to put spirit into women, to raise them from simple animalism.

3 Eva Gore-Booth aged twelve.

4 Eva and Constance Gore-Booth at Lissadell in their early twenties as Yeats would have seen them. Having a gentry upbringing Constance and Eva were articulate and confident unlike Esther who was self-conscious and a tentative speaker. Constance, being sentenced for her part in the Easter Rising, snapped 'Speak Up!' at the embarrassed officer who was mumbling what she assumed to be her death sentence.

5 Eva Gore-Booth, *c.* 1897.

6 Esther Roper as a student at Owens College, c. 1892; one of the earliest women graduates from Victoria University, Manchester, she was misleadingly frail in appearance. She was an asthmatic and unable to speak fluently in public but she had great stamina and application. She was institutionalised from the age of three in Missionary Boarding Schools so that it is not surprising that her life was given to the ideal of community and to improving women's role within it.

E. G. Roper

CALENDAR ✠ FOR 1898.

STRENGTH AND HONOUR ARE HER CLOTHING.

WITH WOMENS SUFFRAGE DIRECTORY

PRICE SIXPENCE.

7 Esther Roper's *Women's Suffrage Directory* and calendar for 1898.

8 The porte-cochere at Lissadell. This was a house built on an enormous scale. Carriages could drive into the porte-cochere through one door and out the other. When both pairs of doors were closed ladies could safely descend and enter the house, without the slightest inconvenience from wind and rain. In 1898 Eva left Lissadell and moved to a little house in Manchester to live with the Ropers. It could fit into the space occupied by the Lissadell porte-cochere.

9 83 Heald Place, where the Ropers lived in Manchester.

THE CASE

FOR

WOMEN'S SUFFRAGE

THE CASE
FOR
WOMEN'S SUFFRAGE

BY

MABEL ATKINSON
FLORENCE BALGARNIE
EVA GORE-BOOTH
R. F. CHOLMELEY
C. DESPARD
MILLICENT GARRETT FAWCETT
J. KEIR HARDIE, M.P.

NELLIE ALMA MARTEL
MARGARET McMILLAN
ROSALIND NASH
EDITH PALLISER
EMMELINE PANKHURST
CHRISTABEL PANKHURST
CONSTANCE SMEDLEY
I. ZANGWILL

2/6 NET

Edited by

BROUGHAM VILLIERS

T. FISHER UNWIN

10 The cover of *The Case for Women's Suffrage* 1907.

Esther's talent was for organisation and from the beginning of her career she was absorbed by addresses, petitioning, leafleting and committee meetings; an endless grind that would have become unbearable without her sense of humour and the companionship of Eva. They were quite different in their way of working – Esther behind-the-scenes, quiet and not given to easy camaraderie but Eva very open, approachable and out-going so that at first in Manchester she did 'make life more truly worth living' for many by her work at the Settlement.

In 1900 Eva made her will as it was expected that she had not long to live, particularly as she had elected to live in Manchester rather than prolong her life by retirement to Italy or Switzerland. She had lived and worked with Esther for four years.

THIS IS THE LAST AND ONLY WILL of me EVA SELINA GORE BOOTH of Lissadell in the County of Sligo I devise and bequeath all the estate and effects whatsoever and wheresoever both real and personal to which I may be entitled or which I may have power to dispose of at my decease unto my friend Esther Gertrude Roper and I appoint her sole EXECUTRIX of this my will IN WITNESS WHEREOF I have hereunto set my hand this first day of March one thousand nine hundred – EVA S GORE BOOTH – Signed by the above named testatrix as her last will in the presence of us present at the same time who in her presence and at her request and in the presence of each other have hereunto subscribed our names as witnesses – J A GRAINGER Solicitor Manchester – F W GREENHALGH 17 Raymond Street Bury Solicitors Clerk –

On the 21st day of January 1927 Probate of this will was granted.

Eva died twenty-six years after making this will. Nothing was changed. Esther inherited £4,262. 12s from Eva in 1927. But in 1900, refusing to be downcast by medical opinion, she became involved in serious industrial organisation when she became Co-secretary, with Sarah Dickenson, of the Manchester and Salford Women's Trade Union Council (WTUC) which was to be midwife at the birth of many women's trade unions. Sarah Dickenson and Eva worked closely together for many years in the greatest harmony. Sarah thought that it was Eva's genuineness that won through what might have been class barriers:

The friendly way that she treated all the women Trade Unionists endeared her to them. If she was approached for advice or help she never failed. She is remembered by thousands of working women in Manchester for her untiring efforts to improve their industrial conditions, for awakening and educating their sense of political freedom, and for social intercourse.

The WTUC to which Eva and Sarah were joint secretaries was a branch of the Manchester and Salford Trades Council that had been founded in 1866 by two officials of the Manchester Typographical Society. Delegates were from all political persuasions. It was a voluntary local pressure group with no paid officials.

Trades Councils had come into being with the recognition of the futility of the very short-lived organisations that sprang up to deal with local problems that fizzled out from exhaustion and lack of any organised central body in support. Sheffield had a Trades Council in 1857, Glasgow in 1858, and London in 1861.

In 1886 the Cradley Heath Chainmakers approached the Trades Council for help in improving their wages. The aim was to raise men's wages from 5/– a week to 13/– and to fix 5/– a week for the women. The women chainmakers were amongst the longest installed in skilled light industry and this demand of 1886 shows us the necessity of separate organisations for women. At this time a young woman starting a career in infant teaching, like Teresa Billington Greig, earned £26 a year which was roughly half the salary of a mill worker, and a third less than a young man starting a career in infant teaching. White-collar refinement had financial disadvantages. A financial report by the North of England Society for Women's Suffrage (NESWS) on funds put aside for organisers indicates a rough average of £50 per annum as their salary, less than the mill workers amongst whom they worked.

In the decade before Eva began work with the WTUC the Trades Council intervened in fifty-seven industrial disputes, and meetings were held monthly from the late 1880s when more notice began to be taken of the claims of women workers. Mrs Paterson had founded a 'Women's Protective and Provident League' in 1874 but it was not until the Match Girls' Strike in 1888 that the subject was very much discussed. In Manchester in this year the Trades Council tried to organise women workers without much success as they were far too fearful of losing their jobs to join unions. In 1889 the Dean of Manchester presided over a public meeting to promote women's unions – particularly in the tailoring trade where there was very obvious corrupt practice by sweating in Manchester, but again this had no success and the Dean learned that women were actively discouraged from attending Trades Council meetings and threatened with dismissal.

So that in 1895 it was decided to set up a separate Women's Trade Union Council for Manchester, Salford and district. The eleven who organised the first meeting included G. D. Kelley (with strong Irish connections, Kelley had Michael Davitt in support when he stood for parliament later), Matthew Arrowdale (past president of the Trades Council), the Bishop of Manchester and Canon Hicks, and on to the new council came the Rev. Steinthal, Miss Amy Bulley, C. E. Schwann MP, and his wife, and C. P. Scott of the *Manchester Guardian*.

Wealthy well-wishers had much to do with the success of the Women's TUC. The income for the first year 1895–6 was £260 from subscriptions and private donations, and by 1901 subs and donations provided £160 and Trade Union grants £21.

The council was quite determined to steer clear of politics and not ally itself strongly with any particular party. It set down its aims as:

1 To promote new and encourage existing organisations among women workers.
2 To collect and publish information as to conditions under which women work, with a view to influencing public opinion and promoting legislation for the improvement of their conditions of labour.
3 To endeavour by all legitimate means to improve such conditions by obtaining for women workers fair and uniform wages, shorter hours and sanitary work rooms.

In the twenty-five years that this WTUC existed it established or helped to establish over forty women's trade unions or branches. The WTUC took a keen interest in the welfare of schoolchildren and Sarah and Eva organised the sending of a resolution to all Lancashire MPs supporting a proposal of the National Union of Teachers (NUT) to raise the age at which children could be employed from eleven to twelve years. In the spring of 1903 Eva became the WTUC representative on the Technical Instruction Committee of the City Council. She had the support of the men's Trade Council and the Manchester Central Council of the Independent Labour Party (that had been founded in Manchester back in May 1892 by John Trevor and Robert Blatchford). Her first campaign as a member of this body was to prevent the exclusion of girls from scholarships at the Municipal School of Technology. This was also when she started to formulate very clear ideas against the 'separate spheres' notion of masculinity and femininity, with its restricted areas of operation, which were to surface again and again in Eva and Esther's campaigns later in the same decade to prevent the 'abolition' of work for barmaids, pit-brow workers and others occupied in work thought unsuited to the 'feminine' ideal.

To the old-fashioned moralist Eva and Esther were 'unfeminine' for speaking in public, encouraging women to be independent and thus disrupting the family, and in asking for the enfranchisement of women. They were working in quite an unusual milieu in Manchester with men who were broad-minded enough to give competent women their head and accept them as co-workers, and with working-class women who were open enough to accept Eva and Esther as friends and mentors.

It is clear that in this setting, to men like John Trevor, and women like Eva and Esther, the words 'friend' and 'comrade' were heavily loaded with a significance now lost; the words resonate with love. What did 'friend' and 'comrade' mean to them? As marriage or maiden-aunthood appealed to neither of them it is worth considering Edward Carpenter's theory of 'Comrade Love' in relationship to them, a theory that he aired in print just as calmly as his theories of rational dress, diet, and the benefits of hard physical labour, and his theory about the type of women prominent in the women's suffrage movement who, he thought, 'do not altogether represent their sex'.

In *Love's Coming of Age* Carpenter noticed that leading suffragists were 'naturally drawn from those in whom the sexual instinct is not preponderant', that some were mannish, some inclined to attach themselves to their own sex rather than the opposite, that children did not interest them and the sexual attentions of men were a 'mere impertinence'; he was careful to point out that he could not say that a majority of them were 'thus out of line' but that a large number were. He does not condemn the fact that these women were 'out of line' and he is one of the first men to ask in print for a re-drawing of the line, a re-definition of women's role, for he continues:

> Certainly those who are freeing themselves from the 'lady' chrysalis are fired with an ardent social enthusiasm and if they may personally differ in some respects from the average of their sex it is certain that their efforts will result in a tremendous improvement in the general position of their more common-place sisters.

He thinks that women will become a 'grander' type by going out into the world and working, becoming independent, before marrying. Carpenter is aghast at the disastrous effects of continual male sexual access to women during marriage. He writes of the importance of 'preventative checks to population'. Miscarriage, infant mortality and gynaecological disease could be avoided: 'Not only man objects to lower Nature's method of producing superfluous individuals only to kill them off again in the struggle for existence; but woman objects to being a mere machine for reproduction . . .'

Sexuality was a great deal more discussed then than is generally realised; non-penetrative sex was a popular subject for discussion and an entire community in America, the Oneida Community, practised it, calling their techniques of love-making 'carezza'. However, Carpenter himself was homosexual and did have physical relationships with men. Describing the love of man for man he asks that 'Comrade Love' be ranked on the same level as 'a great human passion' as the love of a mother for her offspring and the marriage of man and woman. He insists that it infrequently occurs that comrade love is physically expressed by what he poetically calls 'venus aversa' which certainly sounds better than buggery.

In belonging to the group of women who were trying to show others that they need not subscribe to the sexual line, that they could enjoy a free life and choose their way, Eva and Esther rejected notions of sexual possessive love out of hand. Eva connected physical possessiveness with what she called the 'disconnected gropings of self-love'. Writing on 'Divine and Human

Personality' in her *Study of Christ in the Fourth Gospel*, 1923, she said:

> Anyone who has ever felt the sheer passion for impersonal Truth will find it reasonable to think that this passion has its cause deep down in some vibration at the very roots of our being, just as a person, obsessed by sex, seeks his tormentor among the forces in the primary unconscious . . . . It is possible for any man to stop responding to the clamour of animal instinct . . . . 'Whosoever drinks of this water shall thirst again' and it is almost a platitude to point out that these instincts are never fulfilled, and that the more you satisfy them, the less they are satisfied. In dealing with the evils of 'repressed' sex, the psychologists often seem to forget that the logical results of unrestrained sex instinct are disease and death. Not that 'repression' from the outside is the way of life. Christ's suggestion is a quite different wholly active one: 'Follow me,' he said. 'Leave everything and follow me.' There is nothing passive in this, but a substitution of activities . . .

When we read Eva's poem 'Women's Rights', especially the lines 'Rise with us and let us go / to where the living waters flow' with its echo of Christ's 'I am the water of life' we see that Eva very neatly stitched together her love for women with love for Christ and the passage above shows that she felt no sorrow at the absence of sex from her life.

From Eva's poetry it is clear that she was an ecstatic, she did know ecstatic pleasure, but came to it by an intellectual sensualism. Excitement that would be described now as orgasmic in nature, was referred to then as 'ecstasy' or 'sublimity', sometimes 'transport' and it is surprising to discover that two types of ecstasy were common knowledge. Even such a man as Cobden in his *Autobiography* can cheerily give a paragraph on: 'There are two sublimities in nature, one of movement, and one of stillness.' Sexual love was of movement, in time and progressing to a climax from which the process would wind up again; its opposite, what they called 'psychic love', involved a complete loss of self, through self forgetting – not the self-consciousness of possessing or being possessed by another, but in the enjoyment of being with the loved one. This was a 'sublimity of stillness', timeless and ecstatic.

As we have seen, possessiveness was associated with masculinity by Eva, and we find her in her poetry describing the love that is available and not possessive, not sexual, but healthy and necessary to women. Friendship with other women could make them confident, personable and able to look upon the merely sexual role that most men expected of them as too limited and stultifying. In *Women's Rights* Eva calls her listeners away from the round of girlhood, courtship, marriage, motherhood, loss:

> . . . where men in office sit
> Winter holds the human wit.
>
> In the dark and dreary town
> Summer's green is trampled down
>
> Frozen, frozen everywhere
> Are the springs of thought and prayer
>
> Rise with us and let us go
> To where the living waters flow
>
> Oh, whatever men may say
> Ours is the wide and open way.
>
> Oh, whatever men may dream
> We have the blue air and the stream
>
> Men have got their towers and walls
> We have cliffs and waterfalls
>
> Oh, whatever men may do
> Ours is the gold air and the blue
>
> Men have got their pomp and pride –
> All the green world is on our side.

In the first decade of this century there were no 'Greens', no Friends of the Earth, no Greenham women. Eva's was a lone and early voice protesting against the 'mechanic will' of man. On the whole, man could safely put aside Eva's words as the delusions of a cranky spinster.

CHAPTER 5

SOME SUFFRAGISTS BECOME RADICAL

In the 1890s and early years of this century it was only a very unusual type of man who openly supported women's suffrage. In the course of trying to promote their cause in Parliament women found that in every political party that they turned to there would be men with a well-hidden deeply conservative core on the question of women.

If we look at some of the antipathetic male reactions at this time we see that for a man to accept women as equals actually threw doubts on his virility in the mind of the average British male. The Independent Labour Party might have been supposed to be progressive but we find in men like Ramsay MacDonald – who so dismally failed to respond to Esther's claims – and A. R. Orage, the editor of the *New Age* and shining light of 'modern' Labour intelligentsia, socialists whose manliness required women to be what they always had been – confirmers of virility first and foremost.

Both these men owed everything to their mothers. MacDonald was the illegitimate son of a very poor woman, and Orage, whose dissipated father died young, was also brought up by his mother alone – yet social convention supplied them both with fixed notions of womanhood, and neither brought their minds to bear on the subject. They could not see any problem. The sexual *status quo* was perfectly acceptable to them and in the writings of Orage on the 'woman question' we find a very basic sexual braggadocio that leads him to characterise men who were sympathetic to women's claims as 'babies' and 'eunuchs'. We may imagine the deep self-satisfaction that accompanied his writing of this passage – written at the height of the Pankhurst WSPU agitations:

> We have never known a man who was not, openly or secretly, proud of being able to support women; whether they were his sisters or his mistresses. We have never known a woman who did not regard the change, from economic dependence on an employer to economic dependence on a man, as an honourable promotion. What is the good of men and women lying to each other about these things? It is not we that have made them; it is not lying that will alter them.

This accepted state of affairs, that so suited men, was indeed a 'made' thing and fortunately for the women's cause members of the male intelligentsia who did not feel that their virility was threatened spoke out to try and re-educate the Orage cast of male mind. The remarkable Jewish novelist Israel Zangwill was a founder member of the Men's League for Women's Suffrage whose suffrage speeches are still well-worth reading. He had a remarkable talent for introducing the subject of reform of the status of women into every aspect of his life. He was a professional journalist as well as novelist and when he was commissioned by the New York *Critic*, in February 1895, to write a memorial piece on Robert Louis Stevenson we might not expect much opportunity for Zangwill to sound off on his pet subject. But he does. In a fine appreciation of the 'elemental simplicity' of Stevenson's writings Zangwill leads into his second paragraph:

> It was this strain of Bohemianism, this pervasive sense of the romantic and picaresque that gave him an interest in rogues . . . and probing in many a creation the psychology of the scoundrel . . . . That women did not cut any figure in his books springs from this same interest in the elemental. Women are not born, but made. They are a social product of infinite complexity and delicacy. For a like reason Stevenson was no interpreter of the modern.

Very few women in the 1890s were in a positive enough frame of mind to make themselves anew, although as we shall see the Owens College Women's Debating Society were aware of their attempt to be New Women but unsure of their success. Novelists

like Gissing and Wells took to the subject of New Women with
some sympathy and it is deeply depressing that as late as 1913 we
find Orage in a review of Wells' *Passionate Friends* still sounding
the sexual supremacist horn. It is all too predictable that he actually
quotes as an authority Dr Almroth Wright, the notorious writer of
the famous letter to *The Times* that set down the reasons for
women's unfitness and disablement by their possession of wombs.
Orage is worried about women not being recognisable as women:

> To obliterate the natural or acquired distinctions between the
> sexes . . . is for him a kind of duty to civilisation. When his
> heroine, the Lady Mary, talks of living her own life and
> belonging to herself, not only does the fool hero, Stephen,
> assent to her claim to these male privileges, but Mr Wells
> pleads for the view with an almost personal appeal. But such
> chatter on the part of a woman like Mary, incapable of
> supporting herself for a day, is chatter and nothing more; and if
> Stephen were not the 'complementary male' spoken of by Dr
> Almroth Wright, he would have either laughed at her or turned
> and left her. That, I hope and believe, is what young men are
> doing to-day with the apes of the wives of Ibsen's and Shaw's
> eunuchs and baby-husbands . . .

Orage clearly thinks that Wells has un-manned himself: 'in the
course of interminable digressions, Mr Wells exfoliates to marvel,
but he never by any chance drops a seed . . .'

It is possible, as a woman, to read Orage's comments on Wells
with real laughter at such puerile adverting to the proper potency
of the male but coming to the end of his notice on Wells we are
brought up with a shock, for this male supremacist has designs on
what he sees as a woman's only distinction – her womb:

> Mechanical progress, in which Mr Wells superseded Jules
> Verne as a popular prophet, is almost, if not quite, a substitute
> for, and certainly a diversion from, intellectual progress. So,
> likewise, I believe, is the eugenic progress Mr Wells appeared to
> have in mind. The Superman – if I may be sententious for a
> moment – will not be born of woman, but of man.

As we have seen there were many men in Owens College who
were not only never going to re-think their attitude to women but

who were vociferously opposed to any change in their status. In the Spring Term of 1898 two debates took place that present an extraordinary contrast in the thinking of the women students and that of the men. At this stage the women and men still debated apart.

The Law Students' Society and Owens College Union Debating Society chose the subject of 'Women's Suffrage'. Mr Woodroofe Fletcher moved 'that in the opinion of this House the Parliamentary Franchise should be extended to women'. He put the case ably but up sprang the opposition to bury him in a hail of old chestnuts:

> If women had not the suffrage, they had better terms at law; they enjoyed consideration from men which men did not show to one another . . .

> The interests of the British Empire were closely connected with commercial considerations, about which women knew nothing; and that feature in women of indecision would lose its charm if it became a characteristic of general policy.

There was a general fear that things would go terribly wrong and out of control if women joined in: 'Women had a province of their own, and men considered that if they gave women the Franchise and drew them into the arena of politics, they would be endangering the interests of the country.' The most revealing objection shows the fear in conservative middle-class circles that to change the voting system would endanger society as it was by an unwelcome take-over, or at least intrusion, by the working classes:

> Mr Faraday, LL.B., said that women were not fitted for political life; and denied that they desired the franchise. Where the franchise was given to women, only the lowest classes voted when the novelty had worn off.

This remark becomes pregnant when we discover what the women were debating in a room nearby. However, in the men's debate the women's cause was lost: 'the resolution was then put and lost by a majority of seven'. Meanwhile the women were debating 'Socialism' and Miss Green put the motion 'that Socialism is a growing movement and is justifiable from the highest point of view'.

Fully aware of the struggles of Emily Davies and Miss Clough in making university education available to them, the Owens' women were quiet revolutionaries; they came to Owens mostly out of Manchester High School for Girls, quite green, but once settled in Owens they took in new ideas. The biggest new idea was socialism, and Morris, Carpenter and Keir Hardie were seriously discussed. To men who had just failed to give women the vote, could they but hear her, Miss Green was talking rank revolution:

> The industrial revolution intensified the difference between master and man, and the people became conscious for the first time of how degraded their position was. The aim of modern socialism is to raise the people by taking away from the rich that wealth which they have not amassed themselves.

Although Miss Bourne put up an opposition, all the speakers from the floor who spoke to the papers supported socialism. The motion was carried by seven votes, fourteen for and seven against. Noticeable features of the women's debates were openness to social change, acceptance of its necessity and reform of the status of women. Very often in both motions and contributions from the floor speakers would cite depictions of women in fiction as responsible for perpetuating a silly image of women. The author who roused most ire in this respect was Hardy.

On 27 April 1895, Miss Muir moved 'that Thomas Hardy is one of the foremost novelists of the day'. She was opposed by Margaret Kemp who, although careful to do justice to Hardy's 'artistic qualities', considered his mental vision defective and that he was too apt to degenerate into cheap sarcasm ... all of Hardy's heroines were representatives of a single type in her opinion. Here Esther joined in from the floor:

> Miss Roper, at some length, objected to the author as having given no picture of the 'modern woman', an impeachment which the proposer of the motion had admitted, and her objection seemed to find many sympathisers. A lively though illogical debate ended in the rejection of the motion by twelve votes to seven.

Margaret Kemp, a fellow student of Esther's, developed her feelings on Hardy and extended her debate into an article printed in the Owens College Union Magazine. The Kemps give a splendid example of a pro-woman's suffrage family. Father, F. Kemp Esq., donates three guineas to subscription for the year 1902–3 to the North of England Society for Women's Suffrage (NESWS). His five daughters contribute as they were able: Alice one guinea, Amy ten shillings, Margaret five shillings, and the two youngest two shillings and sixpence. Mother Kemp contributes a pound to the Special Organising Fund.

Margaret Kemp's was a fellow student of Esther's, subject was literature. Her published comments on Hardy's depiction of women show that, however uncertain they were of themselves as New Women, the Owens' women students and graduates utterly repudiated the traditional picture of women as weak-willed, passive and victimised.

Although praising Hardy for his great descriptive powers and simplicity, Margaret Kemp enlarges on two faults:

> One is the want of development, mentally and morally, in his characters; the other is the uniform baseness of his standard of womanhood .... His women are, with few exceptions, capricious, selfish and dishonest. Intellectually, they can hardly be said to exist; morally, they are diseased emotionally. They are only kindled into existence by some man who becomes their raison d'etre for the time being ... in the hour of temptation they always fall. Self-respect they have none, possibly because of their absorbing selfishness .... Thomas Hardy's woman may be a half truth as regards even a large number of special cases; as a picture of womanhood in general she is a lie ...

Margaret Kemp is clearly aware of the duplicitous type of woman who barters the use of her body for special treatment and of the impasse in any relationship other than sexual that this brings about between men and women:

> Our social conditions will become rotten to the core if this unconcerned treatment of debased social relations is not strenuously opposed. The best men, the best women, are opposing it; and the first expression of their activity is an outspoken

defence of that disinterested honesty which is as natural to good women as it is to good men . . .

Margaret Kemp, like the mill manager quoted on p. 129 who accepted the influence and truth to life of novelists like Mrs Gaskell in the sphere of industrial reform, clearly acknowledges the widespread influence of novels in all classes of society and is concerned that the image of women given by Hardy should not mutely be accepted:

> The novelist who can manufacture a series of helplessly ignor-
> ant women, whose foibles he then dissects with sneering and
> contemptuous pity, can hardly escape a detriment to his own
> genius and influence as serious and far-spreading in its own
> way as his unphilosophical defaming of the womanly
> character.

We find the Owens' women making a review of their position as women in a very light-hearted debate on 13 January 1898. Mrs Tout, Professor Tout's wife, read a paper in support of the motion 'that there is a tendency in women's education of the present day to ignore many valuable parts of our grandmothers' training'. She lamented the fact that girls specialised in one subject and narrowed their interests:

> The education of the present day with its examinations ever
> looming in the distance, and the later life with its hurry and
> incessant competition resulted, so that it was the exception to
> find a restful face . . . people had no time to be polite . . .

Miss Winstanley's opposing paper shows how quickly and completely rooted were the ideas of equal opportunity. Miss Winstanley's type was the product of less than a generation of women's university education; what confidence radiates from her:

> Whereas our grandmothers were educated purely as women
> more or less on one plan, we in these days are educated, as men
> always have been educated, along different lines and for
> different professions . . . Nowadays, women may choose
> almost any occupation and be specially educated for it . . . that

cookery and needlework as being 'woman's work' should be learnt first is wholly a misconception. A woman's work is that profession that she is going to adopt as a livelihood.

Miss Winstanley's resounding confidence was shared by most of the women at this meeting. Esther spoke to support her. Doubtless many other women's debating societies at this time in other colleges had the same high hopes of women; but compared to the vast numbers of unenlightened women their numbers were pitifully small. To set out on an evangelising mission was to go, as Esther found, on a never-ending journey; but at least she was able to begin, for in Manchester women had put a foot in the door marked 'PROFESSIONS': and here was the largest concentration of wage-earning women workers in Britain – the cotton operatives and industrial workers. Esther was to work with these women daily, from leaving Owens in the summer of 1891 until 1913.

To these small bands of early women graduates the solidarity of sisterhood was very real and important and it was their influence that brought numbers of women to see that they had little to gain by staying in ranks behind 'their' men, divided up into different political parties – indeed the Pankhursts came to use political parties as it suited them. This was a period of intense social change where we do see barriers of class between women go down.

Like Esther, Ramsay MacDonald's wife Margaret stood firmly with working-class women. She wrote to Mrs Bruce Glasier:

The impertinence of these middle-class people who think they are more worth listening to than people who have gone through the realities of life and managed to struggle up to the light in spite of drawbacks in education. It makes me feel 'class-conscious' – only it is my own class I feel bitter against.

Writing about the founding of the Women's Labour League in 1909 she said:

It may seem undignified for the university woman to fraternise with the mill hand and to defer to the opinions of a so-called social inferior, however sensible she may be. But those who are in the movement feel that we are only just learning what Life means.

The university woman and the mill hand was quite a formidable combination, a combination that completely altered the suffrage movement.

After a period in the doldrums, leading suffragists, irritated into action by the widespread response to votes for women – 'Why, women don't want it!' – organised a meeting at West-minster Town Hall at the beginning of June 1893 where it was agreed to set in motion a 'Special Appeal' to alert both men and women to the fallacy of the 'common but ignorant objection to the extension of the Franchise – that women do not care about the suffrage'.

Women's suffrage petitions had been presented to Parliament with boring regularity and equal ineffectiveness for many years but the new tack taken by the Special Appeal was that it should be a petition signed solely by women and that it should cross political-party and class boundaries and be 'An Appeal from Women of All Parties and All Classes'. New officers and organisers were needed to implement it and Esther Roper became Secretary of the rather stagnated Manchester National Society for Women's Suffrage (MNSWS) in August 1893.

Esther brought to the MNSWS an organising ability and a thoroughgoing vigour hitherto not seen in their women organisers. She immediately put into action her plan to involve working women by appointing two working women, with great ability as public speakers, as assistant organisers – these were Mrs Winbolt, a handloom weaver from Stockport, and Annie Heaton, a Burnley mill worker.

Previous writers have puzzled over the fact that Esther Roper, with a supposedly rich middle-class background, should have been the first suffrage organiser to cross the class barrier and involve working-class women. As we have seen (in Chapter 2), in fact Esther – the daughter of a factory hand who had 'bettered' himself by becoming a missionary clergyman – was an ideal halfway-house person, highly educated but of indisputable working-class origin and able to appeal more easily and readily to the likes of Annie Heaton and Mrs Winbolt than could any richly-clad lady of the upper echelons of the NUWSS. Esther's potent example would have impressed Selina Cooper, who came to assist Esther in the late 1890s, and was no doubt at the back of Selina's mind when she burst out in a speech 'we are just as good as them duchesses'.

The NUWSS, duchesses and all, saw that great changes were being wrought by taking the suffrage question into the factories and mills. It seemed a possibility that women might present a united front and all together voice their demand, rather than dissipate their efforts amongst their various political parties, who had so signally failed to take note of them.

With her assistants Esther went out 'to bring the Special Appeal under the notice of the factory women of Lancashire and Cheshire . . . .' The women were visited in their homes as well as at factory gates and a large quantity of women's suffrage literature was given away. A typical pamphlet from this period boldly asked: 'First – why are working women paid five shillings a week and working men twenty five shillings? Secondly – why do working women live on bread and margarine while working men eat beefsteak and butter? – Because women have no votes.'

In 1894 MNSWS organisers were stretched to their limits with meetings leading up to a 'Great Demonstration' in the Manchester Free Trade Hall, attended by more than 5,000 people, and at which both Dr Pankhurst and Mrs Fawcett spoke. By this stage the Special Appeal's collection of signatures had grown so large that Esther had to appoint two sub-committees, one in Gorton and the other in Rochdale, both heavily industrialised.

In a novel move to improve the funding for her campaign Esther doubled the subscription from middle-class women. When Esther took the Secretary's position with the MNSWS, subscriptions from members brought in £200, a sad change from the times in the early 1880s when under Lydia Becker's secretaryship subscriptions amounted to over £1,000 per year. In two years Esther doubled the membership, and then doubled the subscription from middle-class members, so great was the need for funding. Printing bills must have been a major drain on her funds, as Esther and her assistants handed out their pamphlets free.

After three years' hard work Esther took a well-earned holiday in Italy. Here she met Eva Gore-Booth and they formed their inexplicable and instant combination. It is easy to see why Esther would be captivated by Eva who was physically quite remarkable – very tall, with a cloud of straying fair hair and a striking face that had a luminosity that struck everyone who saw her. She was far from knowing her effect upon people, being acutely short-sighted which may have given rise to her benign and attentive expression.

The mill workers and factory girls who first saw Eva when she began to work among them in 1897 all conveyed the same awestruck pleasure that this beautiful person was with them and for them. Sarah Dickenson, a textile worker, remembered:

> My first impression of her was her charming and interesting personality. When I knew her better I found how very genuine she was in all her dealings and discovered all the beautiful traits in her character, the friendly way she treated all the women Trade Unionists endeared her to them . . .

Teresa Billington, again, recalled: 'Talking of rebels . . . some people could be lighted like candles, some needed hammer blows to bring out a spark, and some like Eva Gore-Booth were liquid pools of spontaneous combustion . . . .'

From all quarters comes confirmation of Eva's attractiveness and we are left with the puzzle of what Eva saw, or perhaps heard, in Esther. Esther was physically unremarkable, with a plain and earnest face, and not a confident speaker in public. And yet these two talked together as they had never talked to anyone before. It may be that Esther was the first woman university graduate with whom Eva came into close contact. Esther was among the very first women to graduate and early women graduates had a very special aura that made them stand out in the ruck of Victorian ladies trying hard to be angelic in their houses.

In combination Eva and Esther proved irresistibly interesting to the young Christabel Pankhurst. Their ideas roused her from a dreamy and self-indulgent life (see Chapter 6). Roger Fulford is one of the few writers to give proper due to the initial influence of Gore-Booth and Roper on Christabel. In his *Votes for Women* Fulford wrote of Eva:

> There can be no doubt that this rebellious spirit spurning convention and courting suffering planted ideas in the minds of the sisters – ideas which luxuriated in the brooding calm of Lissadell but were not likely to be found on the more conventional pavements of Bloomsbury or Victoria Park, Manchester. History suggests that revolutionary movements often draw

their most dangerous doctrines and sometimes the most fiery exponents of such doctrines from the lavish, reckless and iconoclastic ideas to be found in a sophisticated upper class.

Esther's Special Appeal ground on, accumulating signatures through the 1890s. She revitalised the campaign in 1900 with a special drive into industrial communities by making a newly-worded petition to be signed only by mill women.

The HUMBLE PETITION of the undersigned women workers in the cotton factories of Lancashire: *Showeth*: that in the opinion of your petitioners the continued denial of the franchise to women is unjust and inexpedient. In the home, their position is lowered by such an exclusion from the responsibilities of national life. In the factory, their unrepresented condition places the regulation of their work in the hands of men who are often their rivals as well as fellow workers . . .

One of Esther's women fellow-workers at this time whose memoirs survived was Selina Cooper who, unhesitatingly, acknowledges Esther's primary importance: 'I took an active part in collecting signatures for the great petition. Up to that time the suffrage movement had been a purely academic one. It was through Miss Roper that this great petition started.'

By spring 1901 the suffragists working with Esther had collected 29,359 signatures and Esther took the petition, looking 'like a garden roller in dimension', and fifteen Lancashire women to meet sympathetic MPs and present their petition on 18 March. It was on the evening of this day that Mrs Fawcett unthinkingly entertained the Lancashire deputation at an expensive restaurant where the women were presented with a menu in French and a choice of sumptuous food that must have done nothing but disconcert and worry them – their dinner companions included Lady Frances Balfour. It is possible that Selina Cooper formed her opinion of 'duchesses' at this dinner.

Priscilla Bright Maclaren watched over Esther's career as a suffrage organiser with great interest, and fragments of their correspondence survive in the Manchester archives of the MNSWS. Middle- and upper-class suffragists had a particular way of referring to working-class suffrage women, a way that strikes us now as definitely 'de haut en bas'. For instance, writing to

Esther about the 18 March deputation, Mrs Maclaren wrote: 'I have been delighted with those Manchester women and so glad that Mrs Fawcett showed them attention.'

But Mrs Maclaren was no woolly and superficial thinker. Much controversy in parliament raged at that time about the desires of husbands, once a first wife had died, to substitute immediately the nearest likeness to the departed, and marry his sister-in-law. On this subject Mrs Maclaren wrote to Esther:

> Whilst only three men were willing to ballot to bring in a women's suffrage bill seventy men are anxious to ballot for a 'Deceased Wife's Sister's Bill' – they want to get that passed before women can have a vote as they fear many women would vote against it – can you bring or get brought forward some things which women can *picture* – they are all so blind.

Repeated petitioning seemed to be having little effect. In the summer of 1901 Mrs Maclaren gloomily observed to Esther of the House of Commons: 'They are simply playing with us now.' Trying a new tack, a deputation of women graduates presented a petition to the Commons in March 1902. Esther was one of these and she was one of the speakers. Mrs Maclaren wrote to Katherine Rowton mentioning Esther's contribution to the deputation:

> How wonderful that Miss Roper could take the part she did with so much directness and ability on Thursday – how superior the women were to the men . . . . What a fine historic escort that deputation was! And you know it has been *hushed* by the Press. I do blame the Manchester Guardian. I have seen cuttings from the Daily News and Chronicle with very unworthy accounts . . .
>
> I do hope Miss Roper has performed her journey safely and is not the worse for all her unselfish efforts . . .

Eva and Esther were to put their greatest effort yet into the by-election campaign in the summer of 1901. The Labour candidate, David Shackleton, standing at Clitheroe with the vocal support of Esther, Eva, Christabel and Mrs Pankhurst, Selina Cooper and Sarah Reddish, 'pledged himself to seek the immediate enfranchisement of women on the same terms as men'.

Shackleton was elected on 1 August 1902 – only the third Labour MP in parliament.

It was in this year that Esther engaged in conflict with Ramsay MacDonald, then Secretary of the Labour Representative Committee, over the problems involved in the funding of election campaigns from union funds where the union comprised more than 60 per cent of women. Esther quite rightly pointed out the injustice of Shackleton's being elected by the use of funds collected mainly from women and then failing to press the women's cause in parliament when he got there. Ramsay MacDonald felt so pestered by Esther during this year that he gave up dealing with her personally and passed her correspondence on to his secretarial assistant.

Disheartened by Shackleton's failure to repay his debt to his women supporters, Eva and Esther, with Sarah Reddish and Sarah Dickenson, founded the Lancashire and Cheshire Women Textile and Other Workers' Representation Committee. Esther's appeal to women to support their next candidate is worth giving in full (see pp. 90–1) – Hubert Sweeney dropped out at the last moment to be replaced by Thorley Smith, a monumental mason, who was easy-going and very sympathetic to women. He worked very well with Esther. His campaign opened in Wigan, 3 January 1906: 'The women's suffrage question is the first plank in my programme. The women who are paying the piper are entitled to call the tune . . .,' he said in his opening speech. Esther seconded him with an able speech and some of her blunt, straightfoward and easy nature comes across in a newspaper account of Miss Roper raising great laughter by saying: 'I wish every man in this room could be a woman for five minutes and then they would understand the question.' This is a remark worth remembering when we look at Eva and Esther's attitude to sexuality as given by the journal *Urania* with which they were connected when they lived in Hampstead. For they saw masculinity and femininity as a superficial, outermost layer, almost as a theatrical costume that could be donned and changed at will and having little to do with the deep central core of personality. Beliefs as to what was suitable to a male personality or to a female personality were very rigid indeed and the boldness of the Pankhurst campaign in making violence done by women a part of quite deliberate tactics certainly made a tremendous impact.

The Pankhurst violence oddly attracted great numbers of

continued on p. 91

Lancashire and Cheshire Women Textile and Other Workers' Representation Committee.

Dear Madam,

May I appeal to you, as one of the Graduates who signed the Women's Suffrage Petititon in 1902, to give practical help in a new and important move which is now being attempted, and which, it is hoped, may do a great deal to enforce the claim of women to enfranchisement? Those of us who have watched the development of Parliamentary procedure have realised for some time that, useful as the ordinary methods of agitation have been in the past, it has now become imperative that we should make a change in our tactics to correspond to the change that has gradually come over the House of Commons. In the days when the private member was a power in legislation our object was to influence the bulk of private members, but now that all legislation tends to lapse into the hands of the Government, the powers of private members have become very limited indeed; so that if a Member of Parliament is to produce any practical effect on any question, absolute concentration is necessary. Our subject is a very large and radical one, and we feel the need of the most devoted and specialized services. For a long time we have been uselessly supported by a majority of M.P.s—a little soul in a great body,—and we think more could be gained by one man absolutely devoted to our interests who would be a connecting link between us and the Government.

The enclosed pamphlet, "A Spirited Move towards Freedom," gives an account of the movement which resulted in the formation of the Lancashire and Cheshire Women Textile and Other Workers' Representation Committee. It is written by a former Textile Worker and Trade Union Organiser.

At the invitation of this Committee, Mr. Hubert Sweeney has consented to stand for Parliament as candidate for Wigan at the next election. This Committee, composed of working women from the principal towns of Lancashire and Cheshire, was formed with the object of running Independent Parliamentary candidates on the main issue of securing the franchise for women, who, if elected, would be pledged to devote their energies to this question, and put it before all others. Mr. Sweeney is accordingly standing on these lines. He is independent of party, and represents the claims of women's labour to political enfranchisement. His candidature is, so far, proceeding most satisfactorily. Several private representative meetings, and one large and most enthusiastic public meeting (composed mainly of working men), have been held, and it is confidently hoped that he will receive strong support from the working men of Wigan, whose sympathies are aroused by this appeal from their women fellow-workers.

The women, however, have been unexpectedly confronted with a grave difficulty. At the beginning of the movement they intended to collect the £500 for election expenses from the women workers in the cotton trade. Since then the difficulties in the cotton trade have developed into a crisis, causing wide-spread and deep distress. Many of the keenest suffragists have been reduced from a position of comfort to one of acute poverty. Some of them, accustomed to earn 24s. or 25s. a week, now only draw 6s. or 7s. Far from any improvement being immediately probable, it seems certain that things must first grow worse. The women are working hard, but find that, under these circumstances, a collection of a large sum of money from cotton workers is well-nigh impossible.

We think that this is a matter in which all women who work in any sphere are alike interested, and venture to hope you will see your way to supporting the movement.

I am,

Yours faithfully,

ESTHER ROPER (B.A.)

---

women to the suffrage cause, who were converted by the publicity but unable to associate themselves with violence. In 1909 the NUWSS had seventy societies with 13,161 members, but by 1914 there were 480 societies with 53,000 members. It was a little world apart compared to the vast spread of industrial unions; back in 1901 Esther Roper in her annual report for

NESWS set out her programme of campaign in the counties of Yorkshire, Cheshire and Lancashire amongst textile workers numbering 311,000 women as against 217,000 men.

Esther Roper, though she disdained the use of force, was exercising great power. Mrs Fawcett remained almost in awe of her and always dealt with her carefully. If we make a tally of Esther's 'power of numbers' we can see that she could whistle up 30,000 signatures for a suffrage petition in 1901 from women workers, and at the time that was three times the membership of the NUWSS. She was one of the very few women organisers to be able to command such numbers of women as the period during which it was possible to do this – when union women and suffrage women were drawing together – was very short. For with the introduction of violence into the suffrage campaign a series of splits in the ranks of women followed, and the marshalling army dispersed into warring groups and raiding parties; the agent of division was one attractive young woman.

CHAPTER 6

EVA GORE-BOOTH AND CHRISTABEL PANKHURST

Twenty-year-old Christabel Pankhurst was at a very low ebb when she met Eva and Esther in 1901. She was the daughter of the late Dr Richard Pankhurst, Labour activist and advocate of women's suffrage. Her mother, Emmeline, was to become a more active campaigner in 1907 when she gave up her post as Registrar of Births and Deaths. Christabel had to assist in supporting her brother and sisters. She had been thrown into a profound depression when her mother appointed her to manage a shop selling 'artistic wares, silks, cushions and the rest' and she found herself incapable of the job: 'Business was not good for me and I was not good for business.' Mrs Pankhurst realised that something must be done to relieve Christabel's boredom and frustration and suggested she 'take' – like a tonic – some classes at the University. Christabel chose to sample logic under Professor Alexander and a few other less demanding courses, like literature.

Christabel attended a lecture given by the Vice-Chancellor, Sir Alfred Hopkinson, on *Poets and Politics* – a most portentous title for a lecture that was to bring about a revolution in Christabel's character. To her own surprise she found herself standing at question time and speaking, rather nervously, but as we shall see, with great effect on her listeners. The Vice-Chancellor was charmed and asked the graduate sitting beside him who she was and then referred to Christabel's remarks in his closing speech. Sitting on the platform with the Vice-Chancellor, as was the custom, was an array of graduates, including a woman who was already known to Christabel by sight.

As Christabel was to cut Eva and Esther, quite surgically, out of her life after 1904, it is a relief to find that she does give an acknowledgement to them in her memoir *Unshackled*, not published until 1959:

> Miss Esther Roper descended from the platform at the close of the meeting and overtook me. She was secretary of the North of England Society for Women's Suffrage, and one of the Committee of the National Union of Women's Suffrage Societies led by Mrs Fawcett. Miss Roper and her friend Eva Gore-Booth, secretary of the Manchester Women's Trade Council, played an important part in the final phase of the suffrage movement. Esther Roper had stirred Eva Gore-Booth to strong interest in the women's cause and the latter left, for its sake, her home in the West of Ireland to live in Manchester. Between them they were conducting something of a woman's suffrage revival . . .

Esther took Christabel to Heald Place to meet Eva; Christabel was at once captivated and threw herself into all the activities of her new-found friends. David Mitchell, like other historians of the women's movement, acknowledges that Christabel served her political apprenticeship with Eva and Esther and, he says, they 'rescued her from boredom'. Like other writers, too, he takes Esther's gentle manner and 'cultivation' for granted as a sign of her 'class': 'The attention shown to her by these highly cultivated gentlewomen flattered Christabel and restored a self-confidence that had been badly shaken . . . .'

Eva fired Christabel with enthusiasm for poetry and she joined Eva's Poetry Circle at the University Settlement. Teresa Billington Greig was also a member – she jotted down as a note of memorable teachers at the Settlement: 'Eva Gore-Booth sybil-like at her Poetry Circle' and made a very acute observation of the young Christabel at this stage:

> Those who knew Christabel the militant planner and dictator may find it difficult to see her as a student of poetry serving in the ranks of the followers of a rebel Irish woman poet and teacher who missed greatness only by external accident of time and of place. But she did serve in this way, just as she sought

and trained for a career in ballet before her mind was turned –
as she grew too tall for this career – to the advantages of legal
training and the drama opportunities of a Barrister serving the
feminist cause . . .

The person who turned Christabel's mind to the study of law
was Esther. Esther had, very perceptively considering Christabel's distracting appearance – light, bright and pretty – and
flightiness, noticed that Christabel had a fine turn of phrase,
quick understanding and powers of retort, and had suggested to
Mrs Pankhurst that Christabel be enrolled at the University to
study law. It is a tribute to Esther's powers of persuasion that Mrs
Pankhurst took this seriously, and that it came to pass.

Teresa Billington Greig hits upon an element in the character of
Emmeline and Christabel when she suggests that Christabel saw
the practice of law as an extension of dramatic art, for self-
dramatisation was a blight on their characters. As an example of
her tone, Emmeline Pankhurst was to say, on one of her many
releases from prison, 'O kind fate that cast me for this glorious
role in the history of women', and many of the Pankhursts'
colleagues and observers were to be repelled by what they saw as
opportunist role-playing which was the characteristic behaviour
that suffragists were trying to get women to unlearn in relation to
men.

Mother and daughter were very alike, and Emmeline was
acutely possessive of Christabel, so that when Christabel began to
change before her very eyes under the influence of Eva, Emmeline
became intensely jealous. Mrs Pankhurst never mentioned Eva
and Esther in her memoirs, so that the only other Pankhurst to
record Eva and Esther's influence on Christabel is Sylvia in
Chapter 2 of *The Suffragette Movement*, 'Women's Labour
Representation – The Women's Social and Political Union
Formed':

Mrs Pankhurst had already hired the attic over Emerson's as a
studio for me. I took up again my old tasks at home; house-
keeping, darning, dusting; wrote window tickets for Emerson's, sold designs for cotton prints and the paintings I had
made in Venice.

Christabel was being coached for matriculation. In 1901 she
had come to know Esther Roper, the secretary of the North of

England Women's Suffrage Society, and Eva Gore Booth, secretary of the Women's Trade Union Council of which Sir William Mather, a Liberal employer of labour, was the chairman. The Council itself was mainly composed of well-to-do people desirous of encouraging working women to join. Eva Gore Booth was a minor poet of some distinction and a pacifist-nonresistant. An elder sister of hers was Constance Markievicz, who at that time devoted herself to painting, but later played a prominent part in the Irish rebellion of 1916, was sentenced to death and reprieved, and subsequently was elected as the first woman Member of the British Parliament, though owing to her Sinn Fein pledge of abstention, she did not take her seat. Eva herself had left home, dying of consumption, as it was thought, to give the few months she was told she had to live to the service of working women. Her aim was culture as well as politics. She formed an enthusiastic class of working girls who studied Shakespeare under her guidance. Tall and excessively slender, intensely short-sighted, with a mass of golden hair, worn like a great ball at the nape of her long neck, bespectacled, bending forward, short of breath with high-pitched voice and gasping speech, she was nevertheless a personality of great charm. Christabel adored her, and when Eva suffered from neuralgia, as often happened, she would sit with her for hours, massaging her head. To all of us at home, this seemed remarkable indeed, for Christabel had never been willing to act as the nurse to any other human being. She detested sickness, and had even left home when Adela had scarlet fever and Harry had chicken-pox, on the first occasion going into hired lodgings, on the second to stay with friends.

Mrs Pankhurst was intensely jealous of her daughter's new friendship. She complained to me bitterly that Christabel was never at home now; my words of comfort availed little. Yet through this friendship Christabel was finding the serious interests she had hitherto lacked. She was now an active member of the North of England Women's Suffrage Society Executive, and of the Women's Trade Union Council, and presently her two friends induced her to study law. Shortly after my return from Venice, Miss Roper and Miss Gore Booth decided to spend a holiday there, and Christabel went with them to see what I had seen.

We should notice here Sylvia's formal reference to 'Mrs Pankhurst', for Emmeline did not like her daughter Sylvia and later grew to detest her so much that she would leave the room when Sylvia entered. But the irrational extreme of her dislike was, at this stage, directed at Eva.

Christabel had joined the Committee of the WTUC in 1901 and at first it seems she happily endorsed Eva's views on the necessity for working women to be part of the suffrage movement. When the Women's Social and Political Union (WSPU) was founded, as we see from Sylvia's chapter heading above, the Pankhursts still had a connection with 'Labour Representation'. But in 1904 Christabel tried to force Eva's hand in making the WTUC declare women's suffrage one of its aims to disastrous effect. From this year to the beginning of the war, Christabel caused the splitting of seven organisations. Eva and Esther were too-long established and had far too many supporters for Christabel to damage them badly. The seceding members of the WTUC merely formed up again into the Women's Trade and Labour Council and the National Industrial and Professional Women's Association, that became affectionately known as the 'Ind and Prof'.

The second organisation disrupted by Christabel was the NESWS. This split over Christabel's use of violence at the Free Trade Hall and it was at this point that the friendship between Eva and Christabel ended. Teresa Billington Greig wrote:

> Christabel's close friendship with Eva Gore Booth must have been coming to a close when I became an Ancoats Associate – for the Poetry Classes were no longer attended by her. This could have been in part due to her law studies combined with the greater assistance she had to give her mother. But that there was a cooling atmosphere was made clear by both. Talking of rebels I said to Christabel that some could be lighted like candles, some needed hammer blows to bring out a spark or some like Eva Gore Booth were liquid pools of spontaneous combustion. 'There might be hope for the earlier two' said Christabel, 'but the third form is just temperament without direction.'

Eva indulged in no such unpleasant recriminatory remarks about this extraordinary young woman who had been so close to her for three years. Whatever form of love Christabel felt for Eva, this was to be her only experience of loving another person intensely and her last connection with equals before she ascended the heights of adulation as the figurehead of the suffragettes. Old hands in the suffrage movement could not abide the new Christabel. The young woman who failed as a shop manager, ballet dancer and friend, who then casually picked up a first in law and disrupted a few unions as she tried her political wings, was not universally admired by women. Helena Swanwick in her memoir *I Have Been Young* wrote:

I felt some admiration for Christabel's impudence and quick wit. She was particularly agile at question time, but her accounts of things had little relation to facts. She seemed to me a lonely person with all her capacity for winning adorers (women and men) with all the brightness of her lips and cheeks and eyes, she was, unlike her sisters, cynical and cold at heart. She gave me the impression of fitful and impulsive ambition and of quite ruthless love of domination. I used to find many of her speeches silly; heaven was to come down to earth, sweating to be abandoned, venereal disease to disappear, eternal peace to reign. Meanwhile she created the atmosphere of a dog-fight. There grew up by degrees the insolence of dictatorship.

We do not know what Eva and Esther privately thought of Christabel's subsequent career, but the initial break between Eva and Christabel came about over Christabel's aggressive and bullying tactics in trying to force the hand of the WTUC. Christabel may have been irritated beyond endurance by Eva's gentle gradualist technique and her peacefulness, never rousing to anger. In connection with this one of Teresa Billington Greig's notes in her material for her autobiography makes a remarkable statement: 'EGB the real inspirer of Christabel Pankhurst in militancy.'

Mrs Pankhurst was waiting in the wings to reclaim Christabel as her own. When she founded the Women's Social and Political Union in October 1903 Christabel was still deeply involved with Eva, but a year later all changed.

The WSPU had to rely, at the beginning, upon the good will of the NESWS and the ILP for publicity and meeting places, but Mrs Pankhurst was a fine speaker, commanding and beautiful to look at – she swung into action very impressively; even her daughter could not fail to be impressed. David Mitchell, in his *Queen Christabel*, makes the suggestion that Mrs Pankhurst had personal as well as humanitarian and political reasons for founding the WSPU:

> Mrs Pankhurst had several times spoken for the NESWS, but one of her main motives was to wean Christabel away from her affection for Eva Gore-Booth. Jealousy combined with reviving political ambition to make the idea of a Pankhurst-led suffrage group urgently attractive.

Here he is only enlarging upon a jealousy already remarked by Sylvia Pankhurst.

It is not surprising to find poems written in a depressed state of mind in Eva's collection *The One and the Many* which came out in the middle of 1904. This is the volume that contains the one Irish poem of Eva's that is always found in anthologies – 'The Little Waves of Breffny' and her poem on Lissadell – 'Lis-an-Doill'. The most arresting poems are a dialogue between the body and the soul, 'The Body to the Soul' and 'The Soul to the Body'. Eva's body addresses her soul:

> You were the moonlight, I lived in the sun;
> Could there ever be peace between us twain?
> I sought the Many, you seek the One,
> You are the slayer, I am the slain.

These are the poems of mourning and loss written by a woman in her early thirties in moderate good health living with a loved companion whose work was fulfilling. Perhaps it is not fanciful to suggest that the mood of 'The Soul to the Body' – where the poet has taken flight into the world of spirit – is connected with Christabel's very public rejection of Eva:

> The lamp has gone out in your eyes,
> The ashes are cold in your heart,
> Yet you smile indifferent-wise,
> Though I depart – though I depart.

> I was the Joy that made you young
> The Light on the moon-haunted sea,

The Soul of each song that was sung,
And the Heart of Mystery . . .

I was the Cloud that made your grief
In the gray twilight of the year,
Now you fall like a fallen leaf,
Without a tear – without a tear.

I was the Force that made you strong
From your brain to your finger tips,
And lifted your heart in a song,
And fashioned the words on your lips.

I was the Hour that made you great,
I was the Deed you left undone,
The soul of love – the heart of hate,
I was the Cloud that hid the sun.

I was the light that made you wise,
I was the Dream that broke your heart –
Now the tears are dry in your eyes
Though I depart – though I depart.

Sexologists openly accused the suffragettes of homosexuality and Christabel defended herself as best she could. She said that she felt motherly towards her suffragettes; they were her family. Their campaign of publicity-seeking and attention-getting rebounded against them in this and adulation of Christabel did go to inordinate lengths; but when we consider the sheer confidence in their mutual love of Eva and Esther, arranging to be buried in the same grave with a quotation from Sappho on their gravestone, there obviously was a socially-acceptable route through companionate love – it was mystic, soulful and not physical. Eva describes *Three Ways of Love* in a later poem:

Love that would have and hold,
Jealous and full of wrath,
Cruel as hate, and as old –
The Love of the Flame for the Moth.

The yearning passion that flies
On the giddy wings of Desire,
The Love of the Unwise –
The Love of the Moth for the Fire.

> Love that is Life and Light,
> Radiance, reflected far
> From the million mirrors of night –
> The Love of the Sun for a Star.

But love relationships that physically 'had and held' between members of the same sex were becoming more common in the 1890s. A feature of homosexual male pairings was the crossing of class divides – there was a tendency to associate the lower classes with warmth and an easy physicality, apparent in the heterosexual world also, and the type of romance in the offing at the end of E. M. Forster's novel *Maurice* came to life for Edward Carpenter when he set up home with an ex-tool grinder called George Merrill. Forster wrote *Maurice* in 1913, fictionalising his Cambridge days at the turn of the century. He was inspired to write *Maurice* after a visit to Carpenter and Merrill who had lived together for almost thirty years when Forster met them; thus he had a model before him when writing the conclusion of *Maurice*.

Carpenter broke the taboo on sex very thoroughly. He published *Love's Coming of Age*, a discussion of 'Sex-Love', 'Woman' and 'Marriage' which appeared first as three pamphlets published by the Manchester Labour Press in 1894. The fourth in the series of pamphlets was printed for private circulation only as it discussed same-sex love; Oscar Wilde's arrest in April 1895 and the dreadful revelations of his trial were rather a setback to public tolerance of such relationships. In *Homogenic Love* Carpenter observes:

> The importance of a bond by which the most passionate and lasting compulsion may draw members of the different classes together, and (as it often seems to do) none the less strongly because they are members of different classes. A moment's consideration must convince us that such a comradeship may, as Whitman says, have 'deepest relations to general politics'. It is noticeable, too, in this deepest relation to politics that the movement among women towards their own liberation and emancipation has been accompanied by a marked development of the homogenic passion among the female sex . . .

Were the middle- and upper-class suffragists allying themselves with working-class women just female Maurices in search of love? Was Eva drawn to Esther because of her childhood happiness with her peasant nurse, because of her direct, no-nonsense Northern warmth and working-woman's style? Whatever physical comfort their comradeship may have given them it is not possible to describe their relationship as 'passionate' – and serious consideration should be given to the effect of strong principle on such women's lives. Carpenter was keen to point out that alliances between women were a matter of deliberate choice and a demonstration that they did not find men indispensable, and far more a matter of politics than the pairing of men, who because of their external sexual organs and simpler mechanisms of arousal, enjoyed frequent genital sex and theorised less:

> It may be that a certain strain in the relations between the opposite sexes which has come about owing to a growing consciousness among women that they have been oppressed and unfairly treated by men, and a growing unwillingness to ally themselves unequally in marriage – that this strain has caused the womankind to draw more closely together and cement alliances of their own. But whatever the cause may be it is pretty certain that such comrade alliances – and of a quite passionate kind – are becoming increasingly common, and especially among the more cultured classes of women, who are working out the great cause of their sex's liberation.

The idea, expressed by the early church and perpetuated by medical men, that woman was purely animal and led man to sin by her sexuality was a long time dying. It was seriously believed that neglect of her reproductive system would lead to woman's insanity and that brain work which was unnatural caused the womb to shrink. No-one pointed out the converse, that continual use of the womb led to brainlessness. Continual use of the womb might lead as well to death through constant childbearing, but, as Luther commented, that was what women were for.

Psychologists and medical men, apparently unaware of any vested interest in applying themselves to manifold 'women's troubles', seemed to think of semen as a panacea for women – thoroughly plough and seed them and all would be well. Young women were rushed into the belief that to be fully 'a woman' they must prove their reproductive systems to be in working order. Marriage was one of life's hurdles to be got over – like menstruation – mechanical and hardly personal. She might be adored, even worshipped, but woman was a lovely animal, flesh, 'the sex' – of a lower nature than man.

The slow dawning of the notion that women were fellow human beings of men – the leading principle of suffragists – began within the female sex, obviously, and the learning of humanity and fellowship was something that women had to get from each other before tackling the problem of how to relate to a man as a person instead of as a sex object, and many suffragists never got to the length of tackling that problem at all; women were enough. The experience of the awakening of personality as independent women was obviously a heady one, and loving relationships between women of like minds became common. This dual discovery, of a mind and speaking it, and companionship, clearly compensated lots of these women for the lack of sexual relationships with men.

In wishing to stress the common humanity of men and women, to stop the polarisation of theatrical extremes of masculinity and femininity which obscured this, Eva and Esther believed that sex, as it was manifested at that time, had to be given up. Inequality in male/female relationships, they thought, arose from the nature of sexual union and its consequences for women. Eva felt that girls and young women were overcome and downcast by being made over-conscious of their sexual organs. She coined a phrase which later became the motto of *Urania*: 'Sex is an Accident' – with no bearing on the essential nature of a human being.

Having these beliefs it was important to Eva and Esther to defend women's right to work and be self-supporting. They were called upon to defend this right many times. Eva was responsible for writing the propaganda of the Women's Trade and Labour Council and in 1906 she wrote *Women's Right to Work* as a penny pamphlet. This was her response to suggested restrictions of women's work – in order to favour the employment of men – in trades like those of the pit-brow lasses and the women chainmakers. David Shackleton had demanded a ban on married women working.

By 1907 barmaids were drawn into the fray by the proposal to make it illegal for women to work after 8 p.m. During the by-election at Manchester in 1908 the barmaids became the centre of controversy, and it was during this campaign, when Winston Churchill was standing for election, that Eva and Esther began to appear eccentric in their demands as, by supporting the barmaids in their right to work, they alienated members of temperance societies and numbers of women whose lives and marriages had been wrecked by alcoholism.

One of the most outspoken critics of the barmaids at this point was Ramsay MacDonald's wife Margaret. She found

> that women were preferred to men because they were cheap
> . . . that women were used simply as decoys to increase the sale
> of drink and to make bars a place of social resort. The
> barmaids had to be good looking; photographs as a rule had to
> be sent with applications for situations; they had to dress
> attractively; in every respect they had to be enticing . . .

Mrs MacDonald thought their employment full of 'grave risk' and she amassed records featuring the barmaid linked with vulgarity, assault, murder and suicide.

But this merely reminded Eva and Esther of the sensationalist frame of mind of people like Principal Greenwood – locking women up for their own safety, and they thought it was a ludicrous notion that in order to safeguard the morals of bar-maids they should be thrown out of employment. A Barmaids Guild had been founded in 1892 by Lady Wolverton, and a short-lived journal *The Barmaid* promoted interest in good conditions of work and pay. Eva and Esther worked with many barmaids – numbers of them were Irish – and good sense and good humour radiates from the 'Bar Interviews' with publicans and their wives in *The Barmaid*. Mrs Hildyard was asked about her barmaids in the 'Old Bun Shop' in the Strand:

> 'You think it a good position for a girl?'
> 'Of course I do, that is if she gets the right sort of place. It is infinitely better than the life of a shop-girl, with all the littlenesses and meannesses connected with selling things in shops, not to mention the insupportable airs of the shop walkers.'
> 'And how about the charges of immorality suggested in some of the halfpenny papers in connection with your business?'
> 'There are good and bad in all walks of life and I cannot say that I have ever heard of such things. More especially is it so in the country where there is not much to do. As for such a state of

things existing in a real business house, conducted on business principles, it is too absurd . . .'

'You believe in giving girls their liberty?'

'Certainly I do. If a girl wants to run wild she will do so, and always finds the ways and means to do it. I believe in giving them a comfortable home . . .'

But it was Eva, and not a woman like Mrs Hildyard, who became public spokeswoman for working-class women whose occupations were threatened; it was she who sharply retaliated to a letter in *The Times* by Mrs Humphrey Ward on 8 March 1907. Mrs Ward was to be one of the founders of the National League for Opposing Woman Suffrage in 1908.

Constance was ever-ready to assist Eva and Esther during any major campaign and she came to help them in the summer of 1908. She had her own unique glamour and the press gave her special attention. The reporting may not always have been accurate but a suffragist countess was worthy of notice. Casimir kept a newspaper clipping, apparently dating from this 1908 visit, that proclaims: 'Russian Countess as Suffragette'. Under a photograph of Constance at work is the caption 'The Countess Marievitchy [*sic*], daughter of the late Sir Henry Gore-Booth, and wife of a Russian count, photographed while painting part of a banner for a women's franchise organisation. She supports the Lancashire and Cheshire Women's Labour Council.'

Barmaids were still the subject of controversy at the great NUWSS demonstration on 15 June 1908. *The Times* report of the working-women's rally in Trafalgar Square shows us the difference in oratorical style between Constance and Eva. They, and Esther and Miss Reddish, delivered their speeches from the foot of the Nelson Column to an audience of about 2,000. The Stepney Gasworks Band was 'in attendance'.

Miss Gore Booth [presiding] said it was not generally realised that there were 5,000,000 women who were earning their livelihood in mills, factories and workshops in the same way that men worked. That was not a small body of workers; it equalled the grown population of Scotland and Ireland put together. One thing, they would find, was always the same and that was that women were not rightly paid for the work they did . . .

Many women were not paid more than six or seven shillings a week at this stage, which was about half a man's wage.

Esther and Miss Reddish spoke after Eva, bringing the subject of barmaids to the fore. Constance then stood to speak. She was a flamboyant figure and a popular speaker who roused the audience to cheering:

> There is a league for the abolition of barmaids, and it is an infamous league (cheers). They cannot abolish woman (cheers), take away her occupation, and let her starve . . . . We are told that the bar is a bad place for women ('So it is'), but the Thames Embankment at night is far worse (cheers).

Seven thousand women took part in the NUWSS demonstration on 15 June. The WSPU Hyde Park rally shortly afterwards attracted an estimated 250,000 which incontrovertibly shows a far greater interest by the public in suffragette activities and publicity.

Barmaids were not abolished, and after that campaign was over Mrs Bernard Drake wrote in the *Women's Industrial News* in April 1914:

> By the shortening of the hours of work, and by the protection of the young girl, the two worst evils are removed as well as the great objection to the employment of women as barmaids. The adult woman claims in the same way as the adult man the right to choose her trade. The remedy for the abuses in the bar is not that women shall be excluded, but that the bar shall be a more fit place for women – and for men.

Between 1908–10 Eva and Esther concerned themselves with the conditions of work of florists' assistants. There was a government enquiry into the hours of work of these women and both Eva and Esther gave evidence on behalf of the women.

In order to bring their women and their claims to the attention of the government they often brought working women to London to present petitions and to process with banners through the streets of London. We find *Times* reports of major processions that included the Manchester WTLC in November 1906, June 1908 and October 1910. The women workers who seemed to have made the greatest impression on London were the pit-brow workers.

At a meeting in the Albert Hall, Manchester, in 1911 Miss King-May and Eva revealed that they had worked with pit-brow lasses at Easter time. Miss King-May, having enjoyed the outdoor work, declared it 'almost an ideal occupation' and Eva proudly revealed that she had been able to push around the coal tubs, called 'tubshoving', with one hand! Sadly, no photograph exists of Miss King-May and Miss Gore-Booth in the coarse, wide, working trousers and headscarves of the pit-brow lasses. At a meeting in Wigan Co-op Hall, Eva and Esther had twenty-one pit-brow lasses on the platform with them, and placards with the slogans 'We claim the Right to Sell our Labour even as our Brothers' and 'Working Women Need to Vote in Order to Protect Themselves in the Industrial World'. Esther spoke a great deal on this subject and wrote a pamphlet for the Men's League for Women's Suffrage: *The Case for the Pit Brow Worker*.

The *Common Cause* reported on a meeting on 12 October 1911 when there were eighty pit-brow women on the platform:

> Their obvious robustness would seem to give the answer to those who suggest that the work of the pit brow women is unhealthy and undesirable . . . . Mrs Alfred Haworth, presiding, said: 'It has been possible to prove that the occupation is not only healthy but that it is conspicuously so . . . .' Miss Roper moved a resolution embodying the objects of the meeting saying she thought it scandalous that men who sat at Westminster to vote themselves £400 a year should vote away the living of thousands of women . . . .

> The resolution was seconded by Miss Gore-Booth who said that while the government was proposing to take away the work of five thousand women and make a large army of unemployed they were bringing forward an Insurance Bill. For men they were inventing a system of out-of-work insurance, and no woman's trade was among those to be insured . . .

On 9 November 1911 Eva and Esther organised a Pit Brow Women's Protest Meeting at the Memorial Hall, Farringdon Street in Manchester. This resolution was passed:

That this meeting demands the deletion of the Clause in the Coal Mines Regulation Bill that abolishes women's work at the Pit Brow. It affirms that there is overwhelming evidence to prove that this work is neither too heavy nor in any way unsuitable, being done under good conditions, short hours [an eight hour day] and very much in the open air. It also protests most earnestly against the proposal to abolish women's labour in the process erroneously called 'tubshoving'. This meeting also demands the franchise as a protection for working women from the present frequent legislative attempts to rob them of their employment.

At this meeting Eva, Miss King-May and Esther and three pit-brow women made speeches. The reporter from *Common Cause* wrote:

The speeches were unusually interesting, terse, packed with facts and full of honest feeling, but the row of women in sun-bonnets and clogs and aprons on the platform was what made them poignant. Here were living witnesses to what men are prepared to do when they speak for women without consulting them. Everybody was sorry the meeting was over. We felt it was good to be with these women . . . . It was sheer insult to talk about their 'morals'. We had met them at tea . . . and they confronted strange ladies with perfect self-possession and the good manners that come from a happy consciousness of being right. They were emphatically 'right' and it makes one rage that some men are anxious to abolish the self reliance, robustness and poise that come from healthy self-respecting labour . . .

Christabel Pankhurst was no longer impressed by the 'right-ness' of women such as these and if she had learned a lesson by the disruption of the Women's Trade Council it was the importance of strong financial support. She saw a new and quicker way to success by the formation of an elite and the conversion of wealthy women to militancy.

Ramsay and Margaret MacDonald were unsympathetic to Eva and Esther – whom they saw as promoting sexual antagonism in the Labour Party – but were nevertheless impressed by their work with the Lancashire and Cheshire Women Textile and Other

Workers' Representation Committee (L&CWT&OWRC). Margaret MacDonald commented upon the militants battening onto the groundwork of previous suffragists: 'These people will claim the credit for everything now and people do not trouble very much to go below the surface, and they will agree that when the advertising began, the work began also.' Her husband wrote of her dislike of militancy:

> She scorned the idea that there was anything in common between 'militancy' and revolution . . . . Her sense of loyal devotion to those who do the real work in life was also outraged by the claims of this one section of the movement . . .

Ramsay MacDonald, though he had earlier been unsympathetic to Esther's claims on behalf of the L&CWT&OWRC and had brushed them aside, had obviously taken her point and appreciated her influence on opinion when he compared suffragist tactics to militant tactics later in the day:

> With the reappearance of the spirit of political Liberalism a whole group of questions was bound to emerge – Home Rule, Disestablishment, Franchise. They were coming up before a single voice was raised in militant protest; they would have attained their present position in the political field had no militant organisation disturbed a meeting or held a riotous meeting.

That statement is something of an overdose of hindsight, for even by mid-1905 Ramsay MacDonald's opinion was of no interest to the militants in the making. Stalling and equivocation from men who had every reason to put forward women's claims to the Franchise hastened a dramatic change of tactics brought about overnight by Christabel Pankhurst.

CHAPTER 7

DIVISION IN THE SUFFRAGE MOVEMENT

Christabel Pankhurst's career as a Fury and publicist extraordinaire opened on Friday, 13 October 1905, when she and Annie Kenney boldly interrupted a meeting at the Free Trade Hall, Manchester – in which Winston Churchill and Sir Edward Grey were speaking – with the cry 'Will the Liberal Government give votes to women?' They also unfurled a banner before they were literally carried off by policemen. Christabel spat at a policeman in order to commit a technical assault ensuring imprisonment. Annie Kenney and Christabel ended up in Strangeways, Annie for three days, Christabel for seven.

Teresa Billington had been entrusted with the task of orchestrating maximum publicity from this. Mrs Pankhurst, delightedly seeing the value of it, declared herself at a public meeting on the night after Christabel's imprisonment 'proud to be the mother of one of the young women who had gone to prison'.

On their release from Strangeways, Christabel and Annie were greeted by a welcome committee including Keir Hardie. Esther and Eva, who had been at great pains to support Mrs Pankhurst during the week, presented the girls with flowers, an act that gave rise to much critical comment from Liberal quarters.

Esther sought to support Christabel at the NUWSS Annual Convention at Hull which happened a few days after Christabel's release by declaring that the prison sentence 'had arisen out of an honest earnest effort' to air the suffrage question. The Independent Labour Party included the names of Esther, Eva and Sarah Dickenson on a poster as sponsors of a protest meeting to support

Christabel. At this meeting it was boldly declared, by Philip
Snowden, that the prison stay had done more for the women's
cause than 'all the continued work of such as Mrs Mills and Miss
Ashton . . .' This was a bitter pill that Miss Ashton refused to
swallow, as we shall see.

Up to this point Eva and Esther looked upon Christabel's
efforts as well-meaning, but Christabel was already well out of
anyone's control, and a coldness had set in between her and Eva.
Teresa Billington noted:

> I was in constant touch with the Gore-Booth-Roper household
> for some weeks during the emergency and found to my surprise
> that there was then no direct communication then surviving
> between the parties, and second that it did not matter whether
> they showed their support or not. *I was discouraged from
> approaching them.* Some ILP friends said that this was a very
> wise attitude for the women's Trade Union they sponsored was
> very unpopular with the male Trade Unionists. (My italics.)

Christabel no longer wanted to have anything to do with Eva –
she had given up attending Eva's poetry classes that had once
given so much pleasure. Eva was concerned with Christabel's
changing character. Although Eva and Esther were heavily
involved with the preparations for the Wigan campaign in
support of their candidate, Thorley Smith, Eva took time to go
and listen to Christabel giving a speech justifying her actions at
the Free Trade Hall. Eva was distressed to hear Christabel give a
different account of the event to that already issued in the press.
Teresa Billington was at this meeting also:

> When Christabel and Annie Kenney were making a series of
> defensive speeches in Lancashire after their release from
> Strangeways – Eva Gore-Booth was at one of these and one
> evening seized me dramatically as we left the platform and
> urged upon me that I should tell Christabel not to vary her
> defence from one meeting to another. Now she is out in the
> open, she said, she cannot fit her explanation to her audience.
> She either spat at the policeman or she did not.

She can't tell one tale in Manchester and another in Oldham.
Dale Spender gives an interesting interpretation of the spitting

incident in *Women of Ideas* (p. 564). She assumes that Eva and Esther were such 'ladies' that spitting was so abhorrent to them that they dropped Christabel on the spot. Teresa Billington Greig's papers make it clear that the bone of contention was not spit, but lies.

When Mrs Fawcett published a letter in the *Daily News* apparently supporting Christabel's tactics, Margaret Ashton – who had made public her opinion that these tactics would 'retard rather than hasten' the granting of the vote to women – finally exploded. Her letter reveals that she, in the old-fashioned Liberal camp, had no notion of the disruption in the Labour camp; for all of the activists had resigned from NESWS, apparently in support of Christabel. In her last report to the Annual General Meeting of NESWS Esther had proudly focused on their success with Labour and working-class women, but avoided mentioning Christabel's rumpus and imprisonment. The staider Liberal section of NESWS evidently made very strong objections felt and Sarah Dickenson, Eva Gore-Booth, Nellie Keenan, S. Reddish, C. Pankhurst, K. Rowton, E. Roper and the Rev. Steinthal all dramatically resigned in a body to form a new society. The disunity in the resigning party was not apparent to the average NESWS member who had not thought the campaign to involve working-class women worth pursuing. Margaret Ashton wrote:

I have read your letter of the 11th inst. in the Daily News with regret and I am sure that you cannot have the facts before you, or you, together with the NESWS and the Women's Liberal Association would have been compelled to condemn the action of these few violent women who have so much injured the reputation of women politicians in Manchester. The disturbances were not planned by the working women at all – as far as can be ascertained – but by a small clique calling themselves the Votes for Women Election Committee and including, I believe, Miss Eva Gore-Booth, two Miss Pankhursts and other seceders from the NESWS which disowns them. The cause of disturbance in each case was the demand to ask questions in the middle of the candidate's speech and the determination to harangue the meeting there and then, if the answer – often most courteously given even at that unsuitable moment – were not to their liking. It was not the asking of the questions that was objectionable or objected to – but the time and manner of it. I may say that many of the candidates they questioned are known to have voted for the suffrage, and the meeting, knowing this, and being met to hear the candidates and not these women in the audience, naturally grew restive. Had they been men they would have been turned out far more speedily and violently than was the case – rough as the handling was in one instance at any rate. It has been most deplorable from all points of view and has made it more difficult to approach the Government with dignity than ever before. If I seem officious, forgive me – we women of Lancashire have suffered much from these disturbers who have spent their time shouting while we have been at work . . .

This letter is valuable in being from an eyewitness of the Free Trade Hall demonstration; it differs from Pankhurst accounts dramatically.

Through this year of 1906 Eva and Esther were to see the result, so well-described by Margaret Ashton, of Christabel's violence resounding through the working-class women's movement to disastrous effect. A 'Sheffield woman and a suffragist' wrote a damning letter to the *Manchester Guardian* on 15 January:

I had paid 2/6 to hear Mr Asquith speak . . . in the middle of his argument on Free Trade, a silly woman got up on a seat and began to scream for his views on suffrage . . . . May I put it to Mrs Fawcett, what she would think, if while she was addressing a large audience drawn together to hear her able arguments on the Suffrage, any person, man or woman, interrupted persistently, demanding to know her views on vaccination or Disestablishment or any other subject.

It is clear that women acting thus, have not the faintest idea of the proper use of a public meeting, and as far as this conduct goes are utterly unfit for the exercise of the Franchise . . .

Eva and Esther were eventually impelled to write to Mrs Fawcett to explain their position. For some months the need to explain themselves had pressed upon them but it was not until after the May deputation to Campbell-Bannerman and its disastrous reception, and after a hearty summer campaign of disruption of meetings by the WSPU, that Eva and Esther wrote to Mrs

Fawcett on Lancashire and Cheshire Women Textile and Other Workers' Representation Committee notepaper (the letter is in Eva's hand and written at high speed):

> Dear Mrs Fawcett, speaking for our colleagues we hope you will not write to the papers and say that (as has been done on previous occasions) the scandalous *behaviour* of the women (who made a perfectly right and legitimate protest in the House of Commons about the Franchise) is to be condoned because they represent not only the opinions but the rough and ready methods and violent conduct natural to working women. There is no class in the community who has such good reasons for objecting and does so strongly object to shrieking and throwing yourself on the floor and struggling and kicking as the average working woman, whose dignity is very real to them. We feel we must tell you this as we are in great difficulties because our members in all parts of the country are so outraged at the idea of taking part in such proceedings that everywhere for the first time they are shrinking from public demonstrations. It is not the fact of demonstration or even the violence that is offered to them, it is being mixed up with and held accountable as a class for educated and upper class women who kick, shriek, bite and spit. As far as importance in the eyes of the Government goes where shall we be if the working women do not support us? These demonstrators always behave like cads and it is very hard to get them to realise the necessity for strong open-air demonstrations and numbers, when they are as anxious as they are now to avoid being connected with futile police scuffles. I hope you will excuse the abruptness of this letter, but you do not know how strongly our women feel about it. It is not the rioting, but the *kind* of rioting.

This letter is signed by both Eva and Esther.

Though Mrs Fawcett was dignity personified she was very approachable and was quite understandably revered. But in the 1890s with the emergence of many leaders and spokeswomen in the suffrage movement it was discovered that women could produce just as fine flowers of despotism and autocracy as could men. The NUWSS was proud of the fact that it was democratically organised and members were actually aware at the time of the NUWSS and WSPU campaigns that their label read 'unemotional, reasonable, will never fly into a passion'. Mary Stocks' memoirs give a perfectly frank, and astonishing, account of Mrs Pankhurst and Mrs Fawcett in rather blunt terms influenced by the intervention of World War Two:

> When I describe Mrs Pankhurst as a spell binder I know what I am talking about, because with many others including so wise and experienced a pioneer as Dr Elizabeth Garrett-Anderson, I was myself spell bound by her. Doubtless the late Miss Unity Mitford would have said the same of Hitler. But unlike Miss Mitford, whose hero-worship led her to accept Hitler's leadership and policy, I was among those who expended enthusiasm kindled by the militant campaign in the service of the constitutional organisation.
>
> The contrast of organisation and method as between the two suffrage organisations was dramatically emphasised by the contrast of personalities in the two leaders. Indeed, one hesitates to apply the word 'leader' to Mrs Fawcett in view of its possible translation into such words as 'Führer', 'Duce' or 'Caudillo', which associations might be appropriate to Mrs Pankhurst but wholly inappropriate to Mrs Fawcett. Never were two women who serve the same cause so wholly unlike one another. Mrs Fawcett was a leader in so far as she was the elected and trusted President of her organisation during the most momentous phase of its history . . .

As we come to know more about the conflicting directions and aims of the different suffrage groups in 1906 it is all the more creditable to all concerned that when the suffrage women massed for the concerted deputation to Campbell-Bannerman they presented a dignified and impressive front line.

The 1906 deputation to the Liberal Prime Minister, Campbell-Bannerman, was a catastrophic stumbling-block to the shaky unity of the suffrage movement. Up until this point, if we ignore the already revolutionary followers of Christabel Pankhurst – 'wild young women' – the movement roughly pulled together, assuming that Parliament would come to see, by constitutional means, the justice of its cause.

The choice of speakers for this deputation was critically important and it is deeply moving to read the transcript of the words spoken by such as Mrs Elmy and Miss Davies – given just a few minutes each to encapsulate their aims after decades of suffrage work. We find among the speakers, in addition to these great names of early suffrage campaigns, the new voices like Eva Gore-Booth and her co-worker Sarah Dickenson, the ex-weaver turned suffrage speaker. We find, as always, one of the Bright dynasty, Mrs MacLaren; Margaret Ashton for the Manchester Liberals, and Mrs Pankhurst passionately threatening that, should this deputation be fobbed off yet again, 'we are prepared to sacrifice even life itself in getting this question settled'. Mrs Watson, a Scottish Temperance Society representative, knowing only too well the effects of alcoholism in the working classes, called for the 'abolition of barmaids' in her speech and here we see the seeds of a problem that was to alienate Eva and Esther from some of their supporters, when they set up their campaign to support barmaids, an eccentric move in a class where the abuse of women was closely linked with drinking. The women who spoke together in this deputation were to go in many different ways after the rejection of this last great effort.

So many hopes were pinned on the effectiveness of this deputation that Sarah Dickenson brightly concludes her speech 'with true Lancashire assurance I confidently expect we won't have to come again'. How dreadfully wrong they were to be confident becomes apparent half-way through the odiously patronising response from Campbell-Bannerman. Mrs Elmy and Keir Hardie, who had to answer this response, were ashen, shaken, but so bravely polite. This was a depressing turning-point for Keir Hardie. The first Labour MP, and founding father of his party, he was to leave it because of its failure to support the enfranchisement of women.

The deputation was introduced by Charles MacLaren – another of the Bright clan. He was Mrs MacLaren's (of the Edinburgh Suffrage Society) son, and the nephew of John and Jacob Bright. He was a rare man, a patient and impressive mainstay to the women's cause in parliament.

WOMEN'S FRANCHISE.

The deputation numbered about 350 persons. The speakers were as follows:—

11 Selina Cooper and Eva Gore-Booth with a L&CT&OWRC deputation to Cambell-Bannerman, 19 May 1906. Selina Cooper was stocky and powerful with a splendid carrying voice; she was the most vital of Eva and Esther's colleagues and the best public speaker amongst them. She became a Councillor and a Magistrate. Married at 31, she bore two children, only the youngest, a girl, surviving.

(Much more like this
They seem to me—

But then reporters
Too can see.)

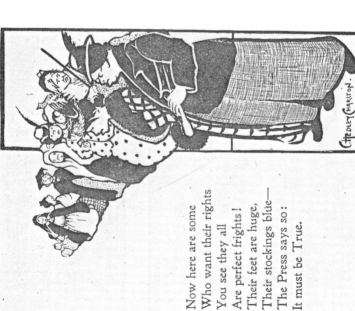

Now here are some
Who want their rights
You see they all
Are perfect frights!
Their feet are huge,
Their stockings blue—
The Press says so:
It must be True.

12 Two line drawings from *Beware! A Warning to Suffragists*, a booklet of suffrage cartoons with a text by Cicely Hamilton, author of *Marriage as a Trade*. It was published by the Artists' Suffrage League, c. 1912, from 259 King's Road, Chelsea.

13 The Round House, Ancoats – a meeting-house used as a rallying-place during the agitation for the repeal of the Corn Laws when Richard Cobden and Feargus O'Connor, the Chartist leader, both spoke here. Manchester University Settlement took over the building shortly after the foundation of the settlement in 1895.

14 The Round House was used by the University Settlement until after the Second World War when it fell into disuse. *The Programme of Events* for 1935 and the plans showing the division of rooms within the building shows that it was a centre of intense activity. It was demolished in the Spring of 1986 shortly after the photograph was taken.

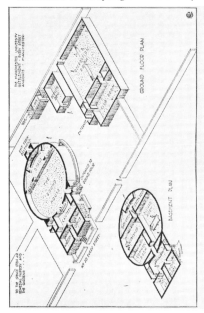

MANCHESTER UNIVERSITY SETTLEMENT.

Residence:
    ANCOATS HALL, EVERY STREET, ANCOATS, MANCHESTER, 4

Offices and Settlement: *Telephone*:
    20 EVERY STREET, ANCOATS.   ARDwick 2915.

Trams: No. 27 from Piccadilly to Pollard St. corner.
        No. 51 from University or Corporation St. passes Ancoats
        Hall.

Visitors are welcome at any time or by appointment.

OFFICERS.

President:
THE RIGHT HON. THE EARL OF CRAWFORD AND BALCARRES,
Chancellor of the University.

Chairman:
PROF. JOHN S. B. STOPFORD, M.D., F.R.S.,
Vice-Chancellor of the University.

Vice-Chairman:
PROFESSOR J. L. STOCKS, D.S.O., M.A.

Honorary Secretaries:
MR. G. ST. C. ROBERTSON.   MRS. MABEL TYLECOTE, Ph.D.

Honorary Treasurer:
MR. J. J. TODD.

Joint Wardens:
RENDEL H. WYATT.   JEAN C. WYATT.

Wardens' Secretary:
MISS GWYNNETH WESTWOOD, B.A.

2

15 Esther Roper, a pencil drawing by Eva Gore-Booth made in Italy, 1920.

Deirdre: Yet [I would] leave Truth I would leave all this and if I saw the eyes of [those] I would dream no more of the songs of the birds. Yea for freedom I would cast aside even the winds of twilight singing gently through the high firs.

Naisi: My brothers Ardan and Ainlee are waiting for us outside the wood. They are very brave, we three will face the whole world together.

Lindri (shuddering): No man can face the past. I can hardly face my own soul.

Naisi: Deirdre do not fear any evil... The voice of Angus is calling to you in the waves and the rising tide.

Deirdre: Naisi I will go with you for surely the voice of Angus has become one with the voice of Manahaun (Lavercam rushes in.)

...that Cathvah the Druid put upon me, that I should cause the destruction of the Red Branch & the ruin of Ulladh. Alas Naisi, I am the bringer of sorrow & the Destroyer of Peace.

Naisi: Nay Deirdre, thou art the Bringer of Light & the Maker of Joy, it is not strange that he should love you.

Deirdre: The King loves me as he loves the forest & the palace & the land that is his. If he found out our love he would slay us as he slays the robbers who chase his deer or the enemies that beleaguer his fortresses.

Naisi: He is very jealous in his love. But he loves you, Deirdre, he is passionate.

Deirdre: There is no Truth no freedom, no peace where there is the jealousy of love...

Naisi: Let us go together, & travel over land and sea & sleep out under the bare sky, and scare the wolves with our campfires & if need be we will look into the eyes of danger & face all weariness & hardship.

Deirdre: Naisi, Naisi, if I sail with you over the seas shall I find Truth & Peace & Freedom in that far country of yours.

Naisi: All these shall be thine, Beloved.

Deirdre: I love the forest Naisi, & the dryness of the dead leaves under my feet, & the rustle of the bracken at my knees, & the shafts of golden sunlight through the young spring boughs, & the thick under-growth, & even the poisonous crowd of hemlock & stinging nettles.

Naisi: There are many such in Alban...

16 A line drawing by Eva Gore-Booth, one of twelve illustrations to *The Buried Life of Deirdre*, published posthumously in 1930. It shows the strong influence of William Blake on her figure drawing.

17 Eva Gore-Booth and Esther Roper with a group of friends, c. 1920.

18 Eva Gore-Booth, c. 1920, probably at Pinehurst School. Both she and Constance preferred to walk barefoot in the country.

19 Eva Gore-Booth making an illustration for *The Buried Life of Deirdre*, a World War One protest play in disguise, in the winter of 1916–17. She is working in her room at the Fitzroy Square flat that was London base for Eva and Esther before they moved to Frognal Gardens in Hampstead in 1921.

20 14 Frognal Gardens, close to the church and church yard of St John's.

21 The headstone at the grave of Eva and Esther in St John's churchyard.

22 The Memorial Window for Eva Gore-Booth installed in the Round House, Ancoats on June 11th, 1928. Commissioned by Esther from Sarah Purser's stained glass studio in Dublin *an Túr Gloine* it was designed and made by Ethel Rhind. Now lost or destroyed.

Sir CHAS. McLAREN: A few weeks ago I had the honour of bringing to you a memorial signed by nearly two hundred members of Parliament, representing every political party in the House of Commons, asking that you would be good enough to receive a deputation of their number to express their views on this question of Women's Franchise, and to express also the hope that you, as the head of a very powerful Ministry in a new Parliament, would see your way to give effect to those views by speedy legislation. You were kind enough to appoint a day to receive that deputation and, more important still, you were good enough to say you would receive deputations representing some twenty associations interested in the political, social and educational advancement of women. These deputations are here to-day; they will be represented by eight ladies who will ask your permission shortly to lay their views before you.

I have only to say this—that, knowing the sympathy with which you have regarded this movement during the forty years it has been before the House of Commons, and knowing, as you do, the intensity of feeling to which this question has given rise amongst every class of politician in this country, I have every hope that you will see your way to do something to give practical effect to the aspirations of those who have this matter at heart. A new spirit prevails in this present House of Commons. We have, largely represented, a Labour party who have come to the House of Commons, not for pleasure, not for sport, but to impress on the public the necessity for action—and immediate action—in dealing with the social questions which we believe lie at the root of this claim for women's suffrage. I would remind you that during the last forty years motions have been repeatedly carried in the House of Commons in favour of it. On the last occasion, when I had the honour of moving in the matter, the resolution was carried, and those who voted represented a majority of every party in the House of Commons; and so we are here to-day, not as Liberals, not as Labour people, not as Conservatives, nor Irish Nationalists, but representing a great body of well considered and influential opinion in favour of this great change. We have to face the question of the social position of that great body of dumb workers who are struggling in our great cities with no voice to represent them in Parliament, and on the betterment of whose lot depends to a large extent the position of the great labour association's, the great trade unions of the country. We think the time has come when they ought to have their claims recognised in the House of Commons . . .

Miss EMILY DAVIES, LL.D.: I have been asked to say a few words on behalf of the Women's Suffrage Societies, whose object is to obtain for women the Parliamentary franchise on the same terms as it is or may be granted to men. In accepting the honour, I recognise it as presumably due to the fact that I happen to be one of the two ladies who had the privilege of handing to Mr. John Stuart Mill for presentation to the House of Commons the first petition in favour of Women's Suffrage. That was in 1866, forty years ago. Forty years is a long time, and during that period great changes have taken place. The basis of the Parliamentary electorate has been largely extended. In 1867, the Representation of the People Act added a considerable number of votes, and in 1884 a further large addition was made, bringing up the total to over seven million voters; but among all these millions, no woman found a place. On the other hand, apart from the electoral disability, the position of women has undergone what may well be called a peaceful revolution. In the early years of the Victorian era the woman doctor was unknown, the woman graduate was a poetic fiction. Now—women can secure the services of legally qualified physicians and surgeons of their own sex and every University in the Kingdom, with two exceptions, has opened its doors to women, who in large numbers have entered in. Forty years ago, it was a novelty for women even to give evidence before a Royal Commission; there were no Women Poor Law Guardians or factory inspectors, or sanitary or school inspectors. Now, women sit on Royal Commissions and receive evidence; and their value as Guardians of the Poor, and as inspectors in various public departments, is widely recognised. In the sphere of practical politics, Members of the House of Commons know well to what extent the electioneering activity of women contributes to the return—or the rejection—of candidates for Parliament. In view of these facts, which I imagine no one will dispute, we submit that the continued withholding of the Parliamentary vote has become a glaring anomaly, in fact, an absurdity. We do not regard it as an innocent survival which nobody minds. We look upon it as an offence to those primarily concerned and an injury to the community; and for forty years we have been pleading for its removal. In doing so, we ask for no special privileges. We claim to be treated like other human beings of sound mind, of full age, and unstained by crime; and we make our plea in faith and hope. We believe that the silent force of public opinion is now more strongly with us than ever before. We are confident that an advance on the part of His Majesty's Government from the stereotyped policy,—dare I say, the unheroic policy?—of bare neutrality would suffice to carry through the moderate measure that we advocate. We look to the sound political instincts of our statesmen, which must surely tell them that the time for this constitutional change has come. We appeal to the courage, the common sense, the love of fair play of our rulers, and we trust that our appeal will not be in vain.

Mrs. EVA McLAREN: The Women's Liberal Federation, for which I am asked to speak, is the largest political body of women in the country.

It has grown from fifteen associations and a few hundred members twenty years ago, to 600 associations and a membership of close on 80,000 to-day.

The figures prove its numerical strength, but it is no less strong in its political conviction and, I may add, in its sense of logic, and consequently it maintains that the enfranchisement of women is the clear duty of a party which claims to be in the van of progress, both political and social.

Miss ASHTON: I am here to represent the larger portion of women Liberals in England and Scotland. I represent nine organisations with 641 associations, and a membership of over 99,000 women, and I am here as their spokesman to-day to ask that the stain of disfranchisement may be removed from the women of the nation. I am instructed to ask in their name for the restitution of those rights of citizenship that we lost early in last century. We accept the whole responsibilities of citizenship; we pay taxes as citizens; we live under the laws; and we obey the laws as citizens. We ask that our voice should be heard in the expenditure of those taxes which are collected from us as from the men; we desire also to influence the legislation passed which we loyally obey. My instructions are not to-day to ask for any particular form of enfranchisement—some of us are in favour of adult suffrage, some in favour of limited qualification; but we leave it to the Liberal party to bring in legislation that will free us.

We are an integral part of the nation, and not the least deserving part. Statistics show that women are less criminal than men; women are less drunken than men; there are fewer able-bodied paupers among women than men. Why should we be left outside the poll? We come to you as the Prime Minister of the strongest Liberal Government we have known in our day. We come as party women who have loyally served the party for many years, and we ask that we may have the promise of your support and of your initiation of legislation that shall give us some measure of enfranchisement. We ask it as Liberals from a Liberal Government, and as Liberal women we ask it from the present Parliament.

Miss EVA GORE BOOTH: I am one of fifty delegates sent by the Lancashire Working Women's Societies, the Trade Unions, and Labour Societies in Lancashire to speak for them and to present their views on this question. What we want to put before you is this. The number of women who are engaged at this time in producing the wealth of this country is double the population of Ireland. It is a very large number. These women are all labouring under the gross disability and industrial disadvantage of an absolute want of political power. Every day we live this becomes a more grave disadvantage, because industrial questions are becoming political questions which are being fought out in Parliament. The vast number of women workers have their point of view and their interest to be considered; but those interests are not considered and the whole effect of their crushing exclusion is to react on the question of their wages. I am a trade union secretary in Manchester, and know from personal experience what women's wages are and the sort of money they get for their work. Six or seven shillings a week is not a sufficient sum of money to live on. That is not a rate of wages that could possibly be forced upon the enfranchised citizens of a free country. We feel, and I think women in other classes, who are working, also feel, that our industrial status is being brought down. It results from the fact that we have no political power. That is the lesson which the working women of Lancashire have learned, and that is the thought they want to bring before you and want you to consider. They want you to consider that they can't wait. It is an industrial need—a terrible industrial need—and the working women cannot go on like this. It is impossible in England with the state of civilisation we have reached that people should continue to get such a rate of wages as this. It is a question which affects us in the most vital way. Therefore, we urge on you to give women the franchise soon. We cannot afford to wait. Poor people can never afford to wait. You want capital to be able to afford to wait. We cannot wait for a Redistribution Bill. Do it before. Do it as soon as you can. I want to urge on you not to put it off to the end of the session to do it if there is time, and not if there is no time, but do it now.

Mrs. PANKHURST: The members of the union I represent to-day are women who are also workers in the organised labour movement of the country. They have worked to create the Labour Party in the House of Commons. They realised that working men needed Labour Representation to protect their interests, and they feel that they, too, as working women, must also have their Labour Representation in the House of Commons. They have instructed me to ask you to enfranchise women this year, either by a clause in the Plural Voting Bill or by a separate measure. Mr. Harcourt has described as a crying abuse the fact that there are men in the country who have more than one vote. What kind of abuse is it that permits no woman to have a vote? If the Government has time to remove the one crying abuse—and I admit that it is—surely the Government should make time to deal with the gross injustice which is an outrage to women. It may be said in reply, first, that the Government has no time at present to deal with this question because of the pressure of other business. We, as women, say no business can be more pressing than ours. We, as women, protest against men going on any longer making laws which we working women have to obey. We also wish to answer another objection that extensions of the franchise are followed by dissolution. We say,—Enfranchise us, make our position safe, and we will be content to wait until we can vote—as the women of Australia did—wait until the next General Election. A growing number of us feel this question so deeply that we have made up our minds that we are prepared, if necessary, to sacrifice even life itself in getting this question settled, or what is, perhaps, even harder, the means by which we live. We appeal to you, Sir, to make this sacrifice unnecessary, by doing in the present year of Parliament this long-deferred justice to women.

Mrs. DICKENSON: As a factory worker for 16 years and a trade union organiser for 11 years, I think I may claim to have some knowledge of the conditions and economic position of women wage-earners. My experience in both departments has shown me the very real need there is for women to have votes. In the north of England men are not the sole bread-winners. Women do their full share of work, with the difference that they have no political power to get economic grievances remedied. Working men know full well what votes have done for them. Working women realise they must have this weapon too, to work out their industrial freedom. That women must live, they must go out to work. Speaking for myself, since I was 11 years of age, I have never eaten a meal I have not earned. I mention this as a typical case of millions of women; yet the fact that women, married and single, are wage-earners and are helping to produce the great wealth of this country, never seems to be taken into consideration by members of Parliament when debating industrial questions. Working women are realising more and more that while they are willing to work, their wages must be kept down because they have no political power. Trade unions will not do all that is required. The real power is in the ballot box. A great agitation in Lancashire is going on at the present time, and women there intend to do everything they can to secure votes. I have just come from Manchester, where there were great hopes among the working women that the present Government would consider the thing in the Plural Voting Bill. We claim that the question is one of the most important nature and should have the immediate attention of the Government. With true Lancashire assurance I confidently expect we won't have to come again.

Miss MARY BATESON: I present this petition for the franchise in the name of women who are doctors of letters, science and law in the Universities of the United Kingdom and of the British Colonies, in the Universities also of Europe and the United States; in the name of those women who have received the honorary degrees of Universities by reason of the services they have rendered to education or learning, or by other work for the national welfare; in the name likewise of those women who are Masters or Bachelors of Arts or Science; and in the name of those who, being excluded from membership of the University, and all the privileges which thereto attach, are suffered to obtain at the

Universities of Oxford and Cambridge a certificate of success in the final honours examinations. It is a petition from women graduates, most of them engaged in the learned and educational professions; in teaching, as professors or lecturers in the universities and in colleges recognised by the universities; in teaching in secondary schools, in training colleges and primary schools. It is a petition from women who are surgeons and physicians; from women who pursue scientific enquiry in mathematics, physics, chemistry and the other branches of science—some of them endowed by Government, by the Royal Society and other learned societies, some Fellows of their colleges or Research Fellows in their universities. It is from women graduates also who are in the Civil Service, working in the several departments of State which accept the service of women; from women graduates engaged in literary or political or social work; from women graduates who serve the State in private life through the work done in their own homes. This petition is presented from 1,530 graduates to show that there are educated women in this realm who believe this disfranchisement of one sex to be injurious to both, and a national wrong in a country which pretends to be governed on a representative system.

Sir HENRY CAMPBELL-BANNERMAN: Sir Chas. McLaren, ladies and gentlemen, I need hardly say that it is a great pleasure to me to meet so large a number of my fellow subjects, so eagerly bent upon a very deserving object. No one can doubt the enthusiasm and determination that you have displayed; no one can question the ability with which your case has been put before us to-day. Every rhetorical grace has been employed, and every argumentative weapon has been used, I think in no case more successfully than by the lady who spoke last, who made so large employment of the weapon of irony—perhaps the most effective of all the weapons that can be used. It is quite refreshing to come here to-day and to listen to a plain and practical question dealt with by those who are intimately acquainted with the needs of the question and with the effect of the present position upon those who are concerned in it. What we have heard on the part of the co-operative societies, on the part of the trades unions, especially in Lancashire, has been most impressive. I have had the advantage of hearing that side of the question before, I think in some cases, by the same ladies, and their advocacy remains deeply impressed on my mind. . . .

... you have made out before the country a conclusive and irrefutable case, and what will tell upon the country is the recognition dawning upon the public mind, the dawn passing as into a fuller day—a recognition of the practical injustice of imposing a disability politically while allowing and even inviting women to share the same circumstances and responsibilities as men. From the Universities at one end of the line to the mill and the workshop at the other end that surely applies. In the battle of life you are placed on the same terms as men, short of the right of effective citizenship. That is where you and I are all agreed. It has been very nice and pleasant hitherto; but now we come to the question of what I can say to you, not as expressing my own individual convictions, but as speaking for others. I have only one thing to preach to you, and that is the virtue of patience. . . . It would never do for me to make any definite statement or pledge on the subject in these circumstances. You have only to be patient for a little. See that you do nothing to hinder the flowing tide by any indiscreet action, because it is very easily swayed in this country. You have the tide with you. Look at the strides made in the last twenty years. I was not in Parliament at the time Miss Davies referred to, but I was there two years later; I have been there since 1868—a good long spell—and I have seen the immense strides this subject has taken, not during the earlier years, but there are years when this desire and even passion for social improvement has taken possession of political parties, and since that came into play I think your subject has advanced enormously. It will go on advancing you may be sure. You will sweep them all into your net sooner or later. It has been suggested that this matter might be incorporated into the Bill introduced against the plurality of voting. I am afraid neither the parliamentary rules of procedure, nor the desire we have for at least carrying one of these two reforms would authorise the mixing of them up. I don't think it would be good policy on your part, and it would ruin the other object we have in view. Leave it with confidence to the growing strength of your case, to the growing impression you are making on the mind and conscience of the country, and if the country would only listen, as we have done to-day, to the half-dozen speeches made by those who are so well acquainted with the matter, I believe it would not be many years at all events before the change you desire is carried into effect. I may disappoint you to-day. To some extent I disappoint myself, but I am obliged in my position to be careful not to give anything of the nature of a promise or pledge, an undertaking, or even a statement that might convey too much to the minds of the public. Therefore, I must be content with giving you this very limited encouragement. But I can assure you from the bottom of my heart of my profound sympathy with the object you have in view.

Mr. KEIR HARDIE, M.P.: I have been asked by those in charge of the arrangements to move a vote of thanks to you for your courtesy in having received the deputation. The case of Women's Suffrage and the enfranchisement of women was never put more forcibly than it has been this afternoon, and I am sure that most of those present, irrespective of their political convictions, suffered disappointment that your concluding statement was not more emphatic. As to patience, there are some ladies present who remember in 1884, and a few years preceding the passing of the County Franchise Act of that year, that the demand for Women's Suffrage was as extensive, as enthusiastic, and apparently as nearly successful as now. By displaying patience their opportunity passed away. I merely mention that, as indicating that patience, like many other virtues, can be carried to excess. . . .

Mrs. WOLSTENHOLME ELMY: I wish to support this vote. I have worked in the cause of Women's Suffrage since October in 1865. You told us in your speech how much we have gained in the last 20 years. I ask you to consider how much we have lost in the last 60 years. What we ask is the restitution of our ancient rights. It seems to have been forgotten entirely that our ancient rights in towns—in the City of London and in many other towns—were co-equal with those of men. It seems to be quite forgotten that, although the Women's Suffrage movement has made great strides everywhere, for the last 20 years it has been impossible to get attention to the iniquities of some of the laws of England. The laws of Scotland are in many respects far better, but respecting the iniquities of the laws of England we haven't been able to take one single step. I speak from bitter personal experience. I have tried in vain since 1884, when we were full of hope. We hoped for everything then, but Mr. Gladstone point blank refused to give us enfranchisement. No Parliament ever offered a greater insult to womanhood than the Parliament of that year. They actually took six or seven divisions on the point whether a felon should continue his disfranchisement for a year after he had served his sentence, but the same Parliament took only one division to decide against the claims of women. Since I began to work, in 1865, I have seen the male voters of this country increase from less than 700,000 to more than 7,000,000. Every increase of this purely masculine vote has made it more and more difficult to remedy the injustices under which we suffer. If I were to tell you of the work of the last 20 years of my life, it would be one long story showing the necessity of the immediate enfranchisement of women.

Sir CHARLES McLAREN, M.P.: There is such a unanimous feeling in favour of Mr. Keir Hardie's motion that it hardly needs to be put.

The motion was then carried with cheers and some hissing.

Sir HENRY CAMPBELL-BANNERMAN: I am deeply grateful to you for passing this resolution . . . . I hope, notwithstanding the little drop of cold water I had to introduce into the end of my speech, that nothing has happened to-day that will not stimulate, rather than damp, your efforts. What you have to do is to go on converting the country as you have been doing the last half-dozen years.

Eva was thrown into a severe depression after the failure of this deputation and wrote the poem 'A Lost Opportunity' at this time, and the remarkable 'Women's Trades on the Embankment' where she compares the women to the wandering tribes of Israel:

> *Women's Trades on the Embankment*
> 'Have Patience!' – The Prime Minister to the Women's Franchise Deputation, 19th May 1906.
>
> Where the Egyptian pillar – old, so old –
> With mystery fronts the open English sky,
> Bearing the yoke of those who heap up gold,
> The sad-eyed workers pass in silence by.
>
> Heavily hewing wood and drawing water
> These have been patient since the world began –
> Patient through centuries of toil and slaughter,
> For Patience is the ultimate soul of man.

Patient with endless lords and overseers
Since long dead Israelites made bricks to please
A King whose heart was hardened to their fears,
What time they still besought him on their knees.

Their patience was the King's confederate,
Their weakness helped his power unaware;
In vain men pray unto the rich and great,
For only God-like spirits answer prayer.

Long has submission played a traitor's part —
Oh human soul, no patience any more
Shall break your wings and harden Pharaoh's heart,
And keep you lingering on the Red Sea shore.

Eva kept two indelible memories from the deputation — one, the image of the Lancashire and Cheshire women workers from the trade unions stolidly marching along the Embankment and the other what she considered to be her own failure:

> *A Lost Opportunity*
> Others there were who spoke with fire and art,
> I stammered, breaking down beneath the weight
> Of that great stone that lies upon my heart . . .
>
> Little I said, who had so much to say —
> This is the memory that sears and stings.

Yet we can read the transcript of the words she delivered — much of her subsequent feelings of failure must have been caused by the flat, bland negativeness of Campbell-Bannerman's response. After this, the drawing-together of women from different classes ceased, and Eva and Esther came to be seen as increasingly eccentric set beside the Liberal NESWS under Margaret Ashton and the flat-out press campaign and demonstrations of the Pankhursts' WSPU; but they were still there. Thirty thousand women, many of them unionised workers, signed Esther Roper's 1901 petition and she continued to have the support of such numbers during and after the foundation of the Pankhursts' WSPU in 1903. The type of working-class woman who stayed firmly in line behind Esther and Eva was not attracted by the WSPU policies and personalities. As the Pankhursts generated such a dazzling limelight about themselves we go into a grey and forgotten area to discover what type of women repudiated the Pankhursts.

They did not have any money to spend on grand dress, though they trimmed their hats bravely. They shopped at the Co-op, and knew the benefits of the Guildswomen's network. They fought for, and won, independence within their families; they had learned to speak up, some of them in public, and a few were filtering into local government. Knowing that they were themselves 'new women' in their class, and that they had become new by their own efforts, they believed that further change via local to national government could be brought about without violence, which they considered demeaning. Through the Guild, the Workers' Educational Association (WEA) and the Co-operative Society they found routes to better themselves.

Just as noticeable as the fact that many of the working-class women in the suffrage movement came from Dissenting or Non-Conformist sects that gave women a voice and share in their services was the fact that they found ways to educate and improve themselves after leaving school in their early 'teens.

From very simple beginnings with a heavy reliance on the barter system, and a 'kitty' of common funds held in trust for the common good of a community, very large organisations like the Co-operative Society and the Workers' Educational Association were thriving by the turn of the century. We can get some idea of the type of self-help and lateral thinking that went on from the start in life given to Albert Mansbridge. Born in 1876, he was the son of a carpenter in a Gloucester village. He became an important figure in the Co-operative movement and founder of the WEA. It all began for him when he was three and his mother sent him to the village dame school with his fee – a pot of jam.

In the absence of the welfare state, workmen (particularly in the industrial areas) found it necessary to band together to protect themselves in times of unemployment or natural disaster. These early unions were called combinations – the word that Mrs Gaskell uses in her novels. If we look at the story of the founding of one of these combinations we can see that they began in a very small-scale and humane way.

When the Hebden Bridge Fustian Manufactory was set up, there was no tradition of fustian making in the area, and numbers of Irishmen who were cutters and dyers were imported from an established mill at Bandon in County Cork to train up local men. In time these Irishmen, who settled happily in the area, became aged and infirm. The local men devised a rota to help one particular Irishman carry his heavy load of fustian from the mill to the stream for washing. One day two young men got into a heated argument as to which of them was to carry the extra load of fustian; the men were obviously expected to remember whose turn it was.

While they were arguing, the old Irishman picked up his fustian and carried it to the stream bank, where he sat down and died. There were no recriminations but the men immediately formed a combination to administer a fund to support the Irishman's widow.

The details of this story were given by the manager of the Hebden Bridge mill, Joseph Greenwood, in a paper that he read in the People's Hall, Albion Street, Leeds, in 1888. Mr Greenwood was an industrialist talking to working men, and after describing the early history of his mill he goes on:

> The period I have stated – 1850 – was not long after the most stirring times of the Chartist movement, and in the midst of the opening up of the Rochdale plan of co-operation. Those who have read 'Shirley', 'Mary Barton', or 'Alton Locke' will better understand the situation.

Thanks to cheap editions and lending libraries Mr Greenwood is able to make reference to these famous 'industrial' novels to a working-class audience in 1888, and the portrait that they give is obviously accepted as genuine. Mr Greenwood refers to Charlotte Brontë's *Shirley* of 1849, Mrs Gaskell's *Mary Barton* of 1848 and Charles Kingsley's *Alton Locke* of 1850.

Working-class women weighed in, too. A pamphlet published in 1894 by the Women's National Co-Op Self-Help Society sets out in plain, tub-thumping words, a new system of Co-operative trading: 'The old methods are due to the power of *money* against *reason* and the cruel power of selfishness as against fair play and Human Brotherhood.'

The Women's Co-operative Guild had been founded by Mrs Acland and Mrs Lawrenson in 1883, and in 1889 the great Margaret Llewelyn Davies (she, of whom Virginia Woolf wrote, 'could compel a steamroller to waltz') became General Secretary, a post she held until 1921. At the festival organised in Manchester in 1892 to mark the establishment of the hundredth branch of the Guild, delegates came from seventy-seven branches to confer and celebrate together for three days. Manchester was the head-quarters of the Co-operative movement and great numbers of working women in the North of England joined the Women's Guild in the early 1890s.

These women were vocal, unafraid to be critical, and proud. The Women's Self-Help Co-op Society pamphlet surges on:

> Just fancy the effect for good of letting loose the pent-up force of *20,000* INTELLIGENT WOMEN in different parts of the country every one of whom was convinced *of*, associated *with*, financially interested *in* and daily benefited *by*, the success of a well-organised, righteous and practical national co-operative scheme . . . to justly claim and get some fair share of God's own gifts meant equally for one and all, to break the neck of capitalistic cruelty and at the same time illustrate the long dormant power of intelligent Co-operative self-help.

The closeness of Eva and Esther's organisations to the Women's Co-op Guild is shown by the fact that their long-time associates were prominent officers of the Women's Guild, notably Sarah Reddish, National President in 1897, and Mrs Green, National President in 1902. It was the Women's Guild that headed the reaction to the Pankhursts' new campaign, centred in London. We can see the weight of numbers represented by the women's unions and the Guild in the report of the joint deputation that accompanied the speakers to the House of Commons to address Campbell-Bannerman on 19 May. Four hundred women represented in person 50,000 textile workers, 22,000 Guildswomen, 1,500 graduates and more than 50,000 members of the British Women's Temperance Association whose spokeswoman was Mrs Watson, from Glasgow. Christabel had come to the point of no longer counting working-class women as a vital ingredient in her campaign. The vast sums of money donated by rich upper- and middle-class supporters had far more bearing on her case now; and compared to the huge numbers of women who recoiled from the violence of the suffragette campaigns the WSPU was a small pressure group whose increasingly rash acts of militancy lead the social historians Jill Liddington and Jill Norris to describe them at the beginning of World War One as 'a small group of outlawed arsonists'.

Dale Spender, in her *Women of Ideas*, seems astonished by contemporary criticism of Christabel, as though Ray Strachey should have stooped to gloss over certain facts in polite silence for the good of the cause. Spender writes: '[Strachey] was deliberately helping to construct positive images of women and women's history. I do not think we can afford to treat each other in this way when we do not control knowledge.' To conceal knowledge of critical contemporary opinion of Christabel Pankhurst *is* controlling knowledge, and whitewash and hagiography are perceptible to intelligent people whether male or female.

It is precisely because people ill-used by Christabel were silent for the good of the cause that her career was unchecked by any overt attacks on her from within ranks. A good example of a pained comment after many years of silence comes from Emmeline Pethick-Lawrence. M. D. Stocks refers to the 'Hitlerian incident' of Mrs Pankhurst's dismissal of the Pethick-Lawrences in 1912 when they had objected to an intensification of the militant campaign. They broke away from the WSPU quite silently, without complaint, to prevent further fission within the movement. Emmeline Pethick-Lawrence, who had been prodigally generous with time and money – as was her husband Frederick – on behalf of the WSPU eventually commented in her biography many years later:

Thus in October, 1912, my direct participation in the militant movement came to an end. The cleavage was final and complete. From that time forward I never saw or heard from Mrs Pankhurst again, and Christabel, who had shared our family life, became a complete stranger. The Pankhursts did nothing by halves!

Working-class women could see that the Pankhurst call for 'Votes for Women' did not include them, for the WSPU was still calling for the vote 'as it is or may be granted to men'. Even in 1911 only 30 per cent of the adult male population had the vote, 6¼ per cent of these being plural voters.

In June 1906 the Women's Co-operative Guild Congress was addressed by Isabella Ford on behalf of the WSPU with little success. Unable to spare the time or money on grand gestures and imprisonment, Mrs Gasson reminded the Guildswomen that their fight for a vote was a personal one to be fought in the home: 'The battle must be fought on our own hearths – with our own menfolk – so that they shall demand equal rights for us . . . we must refuse to canvass for any candidate who will not pledge himself to work for our enfranchisement.'

This is the first sign of the swing to support complete adult suffrage; the Adult Suffrage Society had been founded in 1905, and its first President was Margaret Bondfield, a trade unionist who was to become the first woman Cabinet Minister. Solidarity with their menfolk was what the Guildswomen fell back upon at the spectacle of the richly-dressed WSPU London ladies and their tactics of violent protest.

Although women trade unionists had been prepared to strike, and had organised effective strikes, they would not adopt violence, and it is clear that overwhelming numbers of women in the suffrage movement were incapable of using violence as a policy. On the outbreak of World War One familiar names re-emerge to work with the Women's Peace Crusade and the Women's International League for Peace and Freedom (WILPF), some even repudiated former WSPU beliefs. Mrs Pethick-Lawrence became prominent in the WILPF after her dreadful prison experiences and financial losses on behalf of the WSPU. But that a few women were prepared to be violent in the name of all women had repercussions that must have been unthinkable, the ultimate unthinkable being Emmeline and Christabel Pankhurst's rapprochement with Lloyd George, previously known to them as 'Oily George'. For his oil was such as to still even the troubled waters of Emmeline and Christabel.

A most unfortunate immediate repercussion was that peaceful suffragists had violence directed at them in disgraceful public demonstrations when they were regarded as fair game by thugs and were not assisted in any way. Eva and Esther must have experienced some of this sexual thuggery as a four-line verse survives in a note-book showing that Eva tried to laugh it off:

> A fellow feeling makes us wondrous kind
> Perhaps the poet would have changed his mind
> If he had happened in a crowd to find
> A fellow feeling in his coat behind.

During the period leading up to the First World War the same exasperation with British politicians and their policies that took Christabel to violent revolution was coming to a head in Ireland. When we look down a suffragist's tunnel of vision at this period and an Irish Nationalist's we find the same adamantine block at the end – Herbert Henry Asquith. The Irish Nationalists opted for violence as well and while Eva had been toiling in committee rooms and arguing, arguing, arguing, Constance was teaching her Irish boy scouts to shoot and was preparing to serve in an armed uprising against the Crown.

CHAPTER 8

THE IRISH REBELLION

Although Manchester became 'home' for Eva she returned to Ireland regularly for summer holidays with Esther who looked upon her mother's country quite dispassionately; she did not fall into the trap of the fixed point of view: pro-tenant or pro-landlord. She certainly understood that the Gore-Booths were not representative of their kind. Sir Henry had talks with Esther about the famine years and the effects of Land League agitation, and she was told, with pride, that he had never accepted any police or military protection during times of violent unrest.

Esther was taken over the estate, at breakneck speed in a pony cart, by Eva and Constance, to visit tenants to whom Esther calmly refers as 'peasants':

I was struck by the understanding between both sisters and the peasants. Often when we were out picnicking they would take me into some cottage to tea. I there once heard the story of the Miss Gore-Booths riding at the head of a procession escorting Parnell through the streets of Sligo to some meeting; at which, of course, the conventionally minded were shocked.

This is a reference to an incident sometimes referred to as an apocryphal story – but as Constance and Eva were presumably with Esther when this story was told to her it does in fact seem to tie in with an actual event and probably the first great Land League meeting in County Sligo at Gurteen, not Sligo city, in November 1879. If the girls were there they can hardly have been expected to be showing political commitment at the ages of nine and eleven. But a gathering of 8000 people on their own estate would have been exciting and interesting to both, simply as a spectacle.

Constance and Eva never lost the closeness that they had as children at Lissadell – when Constance came to visit Esther and Eva in Manchester she threw herself into their political work as an extremely effective aide. In return, after Constance had settled in Dublin, they would visit her there en route from Manchester to Lissadell. Even though Eva was a bird of passage through Dublin her poetry was published amongst the literature of the Celtic revival emanating from the city. For example in 1904, her friend AE brought out a volume 'New Songs: A Lyric Selection made by A.E. from poems by Padraic Colum, Eva Gore-Booth, Thomas Keohler, Alice Milligan, Susan Mitchell, Seamus O'Sullivan, George Roberts and Ella Young'. Jack Yeats drew the frontispiece. So both sisters were well-known members of the Dublin arts set. Constance at this stage was known as a painter and actress in the frequent amateur dramatic productions in the city, and it was through the theatre that she was suddenly converted to militant Irish nationalism.

She had been playing the part of Queen Maeve in Edward Martyn's *Maeve* in May 1908 and had idly picked up two Irish newspapers, *The Peasant* and *Sinn Fein*, left lying in the rehearsal room. Scanning the pages she read an article on the trial and death of Robert Emmett which included his famous speech from the dock – she dashed off and joined Sinn Fein and the Inghinidhe na hEireann, a ladies' patriotic organisation founded by Maud Gonne in 1900.

Constance and Casimir were renowned for a brusque, deflatory humour, so that when a society acquaintance remarked that he had not seen Constance at any Castle function for a while, Constance's reply, 'No – I want to blow it up', was merely taken for badinage. During the few years that it took the English establishment and the Irish Nationalists to realise Constance's quite serious intent, she was intensely busy.

Spurred on by indignation when she discovered that Baden-Powell was to bring his Boy Scout movement to Ireland she founded the Fianna na hEireann in 1909. This boys' organisation, funded and dominated by Constance, was to be of prime importance, as the boys were trained to bear arms. In the opinion of Padraic Pearse the Easter Rising would not have taken place without these boys who grew to be Volunteers and the backbone of his forces on the day he decided to do battle with England.

The fact that the Fianna were taught to shoot by an Anglo-Irish landlord's daughter is one of the more bizarre instances of that cyclical exchange of experience that fascinated Eva and of which she wrote in her plays on reincarnation. As so many landlords were shot dead or badly wounded in Ireland during periods of land agitation, men of the landlord class carried guns and their womenfolk were taught to shoot, in the event of armed attack on great houses. Nationalism, then, in Ireland was, to polite society, a thing of imagination and drama, closely associated with amateur theatricals. Had any English agent listened to Constance giving her standard Fianna recruiting address: 'It will take the best and noblest of Ireland's children to win Freedom . . . . Ireland is calling you to join Fianna na h'Eireann, the young army of Ireland, and help to place the crown of freedom on her head . . .', he could not be blamed for dismissing her words as laughable prattle.

As well as immersion in nationalism, Constance took up the cause of the poor labouring classes in Dublin who lived in conditions more appalling than any large city of mainland Britain. She became involved with Larkin and James Connolly, whom Eva and Esther met at Constance's home, Surrey House in Rathgar. Eva and Esther had much in common with Connolly, a union organiser and strong feminist, who had organised textile mill-girls in Belfast in 1911. It was in 1913 that Constance became prominent during the general strike which saw scenes in Dublin of dreadful police violence. On Sunday 31 August, at the end of Horse Show Week, two men died after a baton charge down O'Connell Street. Larkin and Constance were clubbed – she was in the thick of the fray. Four hundred and thirty-three were injured so severely that they needed hospital treatment. This was later called 'Bloody Sunday'.

Constance opened soup kitchens in Liberty Hall, with Hannah Sheehy Skeffington, as starvation tightened its grip on the striking workers and their families. It was by her heroic work in these kitchens that Constance first endeared herself to the poor of Dublin. By late September relief began to come through when the British Trades Union Congress voted to send food to the strikers. A ship from Manchester arrived carrying food from the Wholesale Co-operative Society.

Public reaction to the police violence was extreme and instant all over the country and we find in the speeches of men like Connolly at this period the first calls for some form of militancy. Out of the 1913 strike came the Irish Volunteers. The drilling and training of a uniformed force of Irish troops began. But to the casual observer it still appeared to be playacting.

By the time that World War One broke out late in 1914, Eva and Esther had moved to London for the sake of Eva's health, and they saw with revulsion the onset of jingoism, the constant movement of fresh troops through the city, and the numbers of wounded soldiers on leave. In 1915 at Easter time they went to see Constance in Dublin. Knowing full-well Eva's pacifist views Constance did not speak to them of the ferment of military preparation. Esther wrote: 'She did not speak much to us of the revolutionary side of her life, though, of course, I saw numbers of Fianna boys at her house.' Neither of them had taken Constance's length but neither had the Nationalists or the Unionists; she was soon to shock them all.

Esther shows us how unreal the Volunteers seemed as an actual force:

> I confess I utterly miscalculated the likelihood of a rising. One day about twelve months before 'Easter Week', Eva and I sat in a window of a Dublin house watching the march past of men and women of the Citizen Army and Volunteers, Fianna boys, women of Cuman-na mBan .... There were few uniforms, though Padraic Pearse, their leader, was in full uniform. When it was over, thinking with admiration of all the gifted people in those ranks, I said with relief to Eva, 'Well, thank goodness, they simply can't be planning a rising now, not with such a tiny force.'

Padraic Pearse proclaimed the Irish Republic on behalf of 'The Provisional Government' on Easter Monday, 1916, from the base of Nelson's pillar in Dublin's O'Connell Street. The Irish Citizen Army and the Irish Volunteers combined to form the Irish Republican Army. The Irish forces seized several buildings of strategic importance including the General Post Office. Constance was second-in-command to Seamus Mallin at St Stephen's Green. Government troops converged on the city, 20,000 by Tuesday. The Green became difficult to hold and Mallin and his

troops retreated into the College of Surgeons on this day.
Positions held by the rebels were shelled from the Liffey, the Post
Office went on fire under bombardment and after five days
Padraic Pearse surrendered at 3.45 p.m. on Saturday 29 April.

The rebels were taken to Kilmainham Gaol where on 6 May
Constance was sentenced to death. Throughout the week of the
rising Eva and Esther were frantic with worry – one report
described Constance's dead body lying in St Stephen's Green –
and as all communications with London had been cut when the
rebels took the General Post Office, they had no way of discovering any information.

Constance was reprieved 'solely on account of her sex' – her
sentence commuted to penal servitude for life – and Eva applied
for and was granted permission to visit her. Esther crossed to
Dublin with her on 11 May. Eva had used her influence with a
friend who was a secretary to Prime Minister Asquith. Unknown
to Eva and Esther, Asquith, that large obstruction to women's
suffrage in England, was travelling with them on the *Leinster* and
about to see for himself the situation in Dublin. It was on this visit
that Asquith made his celebrated comment. On noticing that
numbers of the rebels had the most beautiful eyes, he carried on,
'I have no doubt they lied freely.'

The decision of the military court to execute the leaders of the
rising was misguided and counter-productive. Eva and Esther
both wrote accounts of their feelings and experiences in Dublin
immediately after Easter Week and it is Esther who most suc-
cinctly deplores England's vengeful stupidity. When Eva and
Esther had come ashore from the *Leinster* they were appalled to
read on the newsboys' placards 'Connolly shot this morning'.
When they arrived at Mountjoy Prison they finally saw Constance, her face only, through two door grilles, a passageway
between them. They shouted greetings:

Con asked at once whether Connolly had been shot. We had
been warned on no account must we answer this question.
Though no word was spoken she must have seen the answer in
our faces, for with the tears running slowly down her cheeks
she said, 'You needn't tell me, I know. Why didn't they let me
die with my friends?' It was a terrible moment. Under all other
circumstances in prison she kept gay and brave. This was
absolutely the only time I ever saw her show emotion there. But

she had worked for years with Connolly at Liberty Hall, and he was her friend. Also she must have known that he had been dangerously wounded, and that they had had to wait till he was well enough to be strapped on to a chair before they could take him out to shoot him, as they had done a few hours before this interview took place. It was a ghastly story, and for a moment she was overwhelmed. Soon she drew herself up and said, 'Well, Ireland was free for a week.'

After that most of the time was spent in telling us how to find the wife of her Commandant Mrs Mallin, whom she feared would be in great trouble. Her husband was executed, and the birth of a child expected daily. She asked Eva to do everything for her that could be done. She did not think of herself.

On me the notice of James Connolly's execution, the hideous surroundings of the prison, the utter devastation of the streets with their ruined, smoking houses, the terror of the people in the slums, who by now saw a spy in everyone, the squalor and starvation only too plain there – these things made an impression never to be wiped out. Rebellion and revolution are the natural outcome of conditions of life as terrible as those I saw in the slums of Dublin. 'Loyalty' is not, could not be bred in such places. I felt no difficulty that day in understanding why Ireland had risen against England's rule, not only because I am half-Irish myself, but because on the spot it appeared clearly inevitable. Nor could I doubt that more hatred and rebellion would inevitably be bred by such a vengeance as had been taken.

Eva's account of this meeting, published when Constance was still alive, does not mention the fact that Constance cried for Connolly. Esther's account was written after Constance's death.

After seeing Constance they went to Surrey House, which had been wrecked and seized by the military authorities. A crowd gathered, thinking that the Countess had escaped from prison as Eva's resemblance to Constance was so great. Despite the fact that Eva was warned that soldiers might fire on her under the same misapprehension, Eva and Esther then spent several hours tracing Commandant Mallin's wife, going on foot through the streets of Dublin. No information was given to Eva and Esther by the prison authorities as to where Constance would serve her life sentence. After their return to their London flat they waited for news, but Constance's letters were censored; prisoners who had been in the Irish Republican Army began to be transferred to English gaols. An end to their suspense came in a most unexpected way. It was Eva who experienced visions and had flashes of insight, and Esther who was more down to earth, who 'somehow made the world go round'. But for once premonition struck Esther Roper:

On a hot Sunday afternoon in June, we were sitting in the flat thinking and talking of Constance. We knew that at the end of a month in a local prison, long-term prisoners are sent to a convict prison. We also knew that Irish men prisoners had been sent to Lewes Gaol, but we had no news whatever as to her movements. Suddenly, for no reason whatever, I felt I must go to Euston Station to meet the Irish Mail. I was reluctant to say so, for Eva was tired out. However, I did so. She asked 'Why?' I was obliged to reply, 'I have no reason whatever, only I feel I must.' She looked very much astonished, but said, 'Very well, then, I will come with you.' 'No, don't,' I begged, 'it will all be for nothing, I expect.' 'Oh no, if you go, I will go with you,' she said. Mercifully she kept to that. In the late afternoon we went wearily enough. The station was hot and quiet when we got to the arrival platform, and I felt exceedingly silly. 'You go to one end of the platform and I to another,' suggested Eva, and she chose the furthest end. I waited alone, watching idly while various policemen and detectives came along and someone I took to be a staff-officer from the War Office. Then the train came in, a number of passengers emerged, none of whom I knew. I got more and more depressed, when suddenly looking up, I beheld coming towards me the strangest little procession ever seen by my astonished eyes. First a brown cocker spaniel, well known in Dublin as 'The Poppet', then a couple of soldiers with rifles, then Eva and Constance together, smiling and talking hard. Lastly an officer with drawn sword, looking very agitated.

Eva had walked to the end of the platform; when the train came in and stopped she looked up at the carriage that had stopped beside her and found herself looking at Constance. When Constance got down onto the platform and caught sight of Eva they rushed into each other's arms. The officer with drawn sword, frantically imploring them to stop embracing and walk quietly down the platform, did not notice that Constance had shoved papers into her sister's pocket. She had given Eva a document with the names of her court-martial judges, the charge against her and the verdict, all information that had been denied to Eva and her lawyer. On emerging from the station Constance was driven off to Aylesbury Gaol.

Being in Dublin in the week after the rising was for both Eva and Esther a first-hand experience of war. They were revolted by the utter callousness and inhumanity of the military authorities, many instances of which were recounted by Esther in her biographical sketch introducing *The Prison Letters of Countess Markievicz*, but what seems to have marked them most was the personal grief of friends. Hannah Sheehy was the daughter of a Nationalist MP, she married Frank Skeffington in 1903, and they joined their surnames thereafter. He resigned his post as Registrar of the Royal University in protest over its failure to recognise women graduates, of which his wife was one. He became a well-known journalist. Hannah founded the Irish Women's Franchise League in 1908.

Frank Sheehy Skeffington was a fine speaker with strong principles and a convinced pacifist. During Easter week these qualities told against him when he tried to prevent the crowds from looting shops and was himself arrested, and later shot dead, while in the custody of Captain Bowen-Colthurst who was subsequently certified mentally deranged by an inquiry. Eva was to be inspired to write a volume of poems on the rising called *Broken Glory*, but immediately on return to London she wrote a prose account of her experiences in Dublin for a talk given to a society in London. In it she describes a visit that she and Esther made to Hannah Sheehy Skeffington:

> Truly, life is cheap in these days and deaths need little formal apology or introduction. Fresh from that Flanders shambles the soldiers forgot that many civilians have kept a pre-war standard of value, for their own lives at all events.
>
> At the same time, talking to Mrs Sheehy Skeffington that afternoon, one realised there was much more in the story of her husband's murder than mere military carelessness and indifference. Both she and her husband were strong pacifists and they

possessed no weapons, but the windows of the room in which she sat were still broken by the volley fired into it by the soldiers when there was no one in the house but herself and her little boy of seven. Since then the story of her husband's murder has been often told, but at that time the horror of it was still fresh. She showed us the poor little parcel returned from the barracks, containing a watch, a tie and a collar, worthless things, that bore pathetic witness to the almost insane truth – that those who did not scruple to steal human lives were yet most honourable and honest in their dealings with property – to them a much more important matter.

Hearing Mrs Skeffington talk, one realised that though her husband never had a weapon in his hand, militarism was wise in its generation, and in Sheehy Skeffington militarism had struck down its worst enemy – unarmed yet insurgent Idealism.

Constance was to become inured to prison life. She learned a great deal there including Irish – her first stretch in prison lasted from the end of Easter week 1916 to 18 June 1917. The exchange of letters between herself and Eva was life to her; they made an arrangement to communicate telepathically at a particular hour each day, an apparently successful and repeated exercise in thought transference. It is to this that Eva refers in the poem written for Constance called *Comrades*:

COMRADES

The peaceful night that round me flows,
Breaks through your iron prison doors,
Free through the world your spirit goes,
Forbidden hands are clasping yours.

The wind is our confederate,
The night has left her doors ajar,
We meet beyond earth's barred gate,
Where all the world's wild Rebels are.

Constance was kept in what amounted to solitary confinement in Lewes Gaol and Eva and Esther petitioned long and hard for alleviation of the conditions of the Irish prisoners. Esther hated prisons:

> That most dreary spot on earth – a prison. To me it is a misery to enter one, though I have visited many in my time . . . . I ask myself how in Heaven's name shutting out the sun, the wind and the sight of the trees could make a rebel loyal or a thief honest – or indeed do anything but fill the heart with bitterness and hatred of all mankind . . . . I marvel at the patience and courage with which a fiery soul like Constance's went through the ordeal and learned from life before the end, as she did, the lesson of love and pity.

Constance had wanted to die with her comrades-in-arms in Easter week and the curious, very uncharacteristic patience that came upon her after being rescued from this fate assorts with her worn and resigned features in later photographs. She kept her spirits while in prison largely because of Eva who did her utmost to sustain her sister:

TO C.M. ON HER PRISON BIRTHDAY
February 1917

> What has time to do with thee,
> Who hast found the victor's way
> To be rich in poverty,
> Without sunshine to be gay,
> To be free in a prison cell?
> Nay on that undreamed judgement day,
> When on the old world's scrap-heap flung,
> Powers and empires pass away,
> Radiant and unconquerable
> Thou shalt be young.

Much of Eva's poetry written at this period is full of horror at militarism, the triumph of mindless violent aggression and the loss of Christ. Again she is aghast at men:

> Men drench the green earth and defile her streams
> With blood, and blast her very fields and hills
> With the mechanic iron of their wills,
> Yet in her sad heart still the spirit dreams.

In a striking, simply-constructed poem, *The World's Grief*, she savages the mutual forgetfulness of Christ and man and lists the triumphs of ill-nature:

THE WORLD'S GRIEF

'In all earthly happenings
Claws are better far than wings –
Force has dug the grave of Love,'
Said the Tiger to the Dove.

'A little venom on the tongue
Beats any song that e'er was sung –
Great are lies and shall prevail,'
Said the Snake to the Nightingale.

'Always with the great pack fight,
For the pack is always right –
Oh, be loyal if you can,'
Said the Wolf unto the Man.

'For every good under the sun
Man must fight with sword or gun –
Woe to the gentle and the mild,'
Said Man to the human Child.

'In the war of right and wrong
The victory is to the strong –
Great guns must clear your darkened sky,'
Said Man to the Lord Most High.

The moon turned pale, the stars stood still,
'Peace upon earth, to men good will,'
The Angel to the Shepherd cried.
Christ turned in His sleep and sighed.

The Irishmen who gave their lives in Easter week and its aftermath, especially those freakish non-combatant casualties Francis Sheehy Skeffington and Roger Casement, were heroic to Eva and she repeatedly associated both men with Christ in her poems. Naming Sheehy Skeffington 'A leader in the war that shall end war' – unarmed – she wrote for him a pacifist's epitaph.

FRANCIS SHEEHY-SKEFFINGTON

Dublin, April 26, 1916

No green and poisonous laurel wreath shall shade
His brow, who dealt no death in any strife,
Crown him with olive who was not afraid
To join the desolate unarmed ranks of life.

Who did not fear to die, yet feared to slay,
A leader in the war that shall end war,
Unarmed he stood in ruthless Empire's way,
Unarmed he stands on Acheron's lost shore.

Yet not alone, nor all unrecognized,
For at his side does that scorned Dreamer stand,
Who in the Olive Garden agonized,
Whose Kingdom yet shall come in every land.

When driven men, who fight and hate and kill
To order, shall let all their weapons fall,
And know that kindly freedom of the will
That holds no other human will in thrall.

Sir Roger Casement, an Irishman in British diplomatic service overseas, had been knighted in recognition of his work in the Congo, during which he had exposed slave-trading and had become well-known for his humanitarian concerns. He had been converted to Irish nationalism and the necessity of an armed uprising. He promoted an Irish alliance with Germany and in the first years of World War One began to form an Irish Brigade from disaffected Irishmen serving in the British Army who were held in German prisoner of war camps.

A planned delivery of arms from Germany to supply the Irish forces was bungled, and Casement landed himself, on Banna Strand in Kerry, to call off the rising in order to wait on a better opportunity. He was captured on Good Friday and eventually taken to London and tried for treason. The lawyers Gavan Duffy and T. M. Healy, who had helped Constance at her trial, set themselves to make a defence for Casement. Their choice of defence lawyer was unfortunate. They chose Gavan Duffy's brother-in-law, Serjeant Sullivan, who was the last Queen's Serjeant in Ireland. Aged forty-five at the time of the Casement trial, he had decided to leave Ireland and practise in England as he disliked the turn of events in Ireland. Many members of the Irish Bar were ultra-conservative and supporters of the link with England – two characteristics that ensured a deepening gulf between Sullivan and Casement as the revelations of the trial in private consultation and courtroom began.

Casement's cousin, Gertrude Bannister, and the historian Alice Stopford Green tried to rally support for him. Eva was asked to accompany them to the court proceedings as they thought Casement would be cheered by the presence of friends. Eva protested that as she and Casement had never met she would hate to create the impression of being a mere curious sightseer, but Gertrude Bannister insisted that she would be good for Casement. She was right, for as Casement was brought into the dock he bowed to the judge and looked up to see Eva, in the public gallery, who had risen as he came in. They exchanged radiant smiles. Whatever form of recognition took place between them they both felt a strong personal bond. Casement referred to Eva by name in his letters to Gertrude Bannister. That night he wrote: 'Give my love to Eva. I thought her looking so tired in Court to-day.' Casement was a handsome and magnetic man whose proud bearing and relaxed gentle manners during his trial made a great impresson. Gertrude Bannister, perhaps slightly bemused by the obvious attraction between Eva and Casement, thought the 'little half-affair' came about because both of them were mystics.

Eva proceeded to use every waking moment on Casement's behalf. Through her friend H. W. Nevinson, the war-correspondent of the *Manchester Guardian*, and C. P. Scott, its editor, she organised press support for Casement. He needed such support, as his relations with Serjeant Sullivan were worsening. Extraordinarily, but possibly because of his culture's high valuation of oratory and the word, Sullivan had decided to base his entire defence on a point of grammar. The grammar was in a Statute of Edward III of 1351; Sullivan's argument maintained that Casement was not 'within the realm' at the time of his offence against it. In court this boiled down to palaeography – was there or was there not a comma? Could it be a fold in the parchment?

Esther was horrified:

To hear responsible men blandly discussing the placing of a comma in an ancient document as a point on which the life of a human being, in their very presence, might depend; to hear jokes made; to feel that gorgeous raiment was valued as contributing to 'the dignity of the law' – all this was to an ordinary mortal terrible . . .

Casement felt much the same, writing to his friend Richard Morton: 'God deliver me, I say, from such antiquaries as these to hang a man's life upon a comma and throttle him with a semi-colon.'

The British establishment, deeply offended by Casement's turn against the State in organising German aid to Ireland, wished to bring down Casement, and fearing that patriotism and Casement's evident sincerity might impress the jury they used Casement's homosexuality against him to tip the balance decisively. A press campaign villifying Casement as not only a traitor but a pervert was under way with the release of copies of diaries revealing Casement's sexual activities.

Casement had kept his sexuality a secret from his family and friends who were never able to accept that the diaries were genuine; the pro-Casement campaign insisted that the diaries were forged. Eva, Esther and Gertrude Bannister were among those who sincerely believed that the British Government forged the diaries in order to destroy Casement. Gertrude wrote to explain the situation to Casement's sister Nina, describing the diaries as 'lying propaganda', and Esther wrote:

Relentless foes sat in seats of power and they poisoned the public mind by circulating lying stories (that had nothing to do with the case) against the personal character of Roger Casement. Only those who did not know him believed them, and it was a vile way of hunting a man to death.

Casement, questioned by Sullivan as to the authorship of the diaries, confessed to his homosexuality and made an eloquent defence of it. Sullivan was terribly distressed. His accounts of this meeting vary – he was an accomplished *raconteur* – but the outcome was that in delivering his final speech for the defence he blacked out and collapsed. He should have resigned from the case, if his statement in *The Last Serjeant*, his memoirs, reflects his opinion at the time of the trial:

Casement was not completely normal and one of the abnormalities of his type is addiction to lamentable practices. He had the further affliction of the craving to record erotica and this horrible document was in the hands of the Crown.

The uselessness of Serjeant Sullivan inspired Casement's friends to redouble their efforts to get a reprieve. They organised an appeal petition that was signed by many distinguished people. Eva, single-handed, made out the case that Casement had come to stop the rising, not to join it, a point that had never been made at the trial as Casement would not co-operate. Eva wrote later, after the failure of all their efforts:

People on this side of the Channel could not believe that an Irishman would rather be hung than state publicly that he had tried to stop the Sinn Fein rising, and so seem to blame his fellow countrymen in their failure and defeat.

On 2 August, in one last desperate attempt, Gertrude Bannister, Mrs Green, Eva, H. W. Nevinson and Philip Morrell had an audience with the King at Buckingham Palace to plead for clemency, only to be told that the King's Right was now vested in his ministers and he was powerless to act. He could only inform his ministers that he had been appealed to, which he did.

Roger Casement was hung at Pentonville Prison early in the morning of 3 August 1916. A large crowd had gathered to cheer and celebrate as the execution was carried out. At that moment, Casement's friends dropped to their knees on the pavement and began praying for him, Eva with tears streaming down her face. The crowd became silent.

Casement's body was buried in lime as was the prison custom to speed decomposition and a quick turnover of burials in a small area. In her poem *Heroic Death*, 1916, Eva refers to Casement's 'burning grave at Pentonville' – the leaders shot in the prison yard at Kilmainham were buried in the same way.

Three of her poems in *Broken Glory* are for Casement:

GOVERNMENT

The rulers of the earth, savage and blind,
Have dug Gethsemane for all mankind.

For their honour and their glory and their pride,
In every age the heroes of all nations died.
Thus Joan of Arc and Socrates were slain
By the world's bane,
Jesus Christ a thousand years ago,
They served so,
And Roger Casement, just the other day,
Went the same way.
Now is their hour of power and life's despair
From blasted earth and desecrated air
The universal death that is their dream
Flows o'er the earth . . .

Eva suffered a physical decline after the emotional shock of 1916, but the poetess Dora Sigerson Shorter, who suffered the same type of decline, died. Eva wrote a poem in her memory lamenting that she had 'died of the grief that tore my heart' and 'your death from the root of my sorrow grew'.

Eva's poems that spring from actual events or personalities, are very different from her mystic rambles. She concentrates in a small space and expresses her line of thought in a striking way. Easter week and its aftermath prompted many of these short poems.

EASTER WEEK

Grief for the noble dead
Of one who did not share their strife
And mourned that any blood was shed,
Yet felt the broken glory of their state,
Their strange heroic questioning of Fate
Ribbon with gold the rags of this our life.

As well as visiting Constance in her various gaols Eva and Esther spent the last two years of the war attending trials of conscientious objectors for the No-Conscription Fellowship and by 1919 both of them were physically run ragged. They spent 1920 trying to recover health in Italy but they never returned to full lives in active politics, as Eva in particular could not regain full health, and a long, semi-invalid decline set in.

CHAPTER 9

LAST WRITINGS: THE GOSPEL OF LOVE AND *URANIA*

In her last years Eva had become increasingly absorbed in study of the Greek New Testament. The development of her religious beliefs had been quite unexpected. As we know from her *Inner Life of a Child*, even before her teens she had become, in Christian terms, godless and her wide and jumbled reading via the Greeks, William Morris sagas and Swinburne brought her only to a vague pantheism. Contact with AE, as for so many others, led to her study of Eastern mysticism and doctrines of reincarnation. It was reincarnation that enabled her to grasp the possibility that love, as a perfect understanding of another's being, involved an acceptance of complete loss and change of self. Having accepted the change-of-self chain of exchange involved in reincarnation down the ages, Eva took a further step in believing that it was possible in one's daily life, by imaginative pity, to become another person by loving them; and here she came back to the personality of Christ, whom she understood to embody this perfect love.

But she did not come back to the personality of Christ without having fallen into a popular movement of the time. She had become a theosophist, and some of the quotations in this chapter will come from her addresses to the Hampstead Theosophical Society, of which she was a member until her death.

Theosophy had its lunatic fringe and Madame Blavatsky, the high priestess of the movement, had done much damage when she was exposed as a trickster in 1885 by the Society for Psychical Research. Blavatsky's headquarters were in India, the Theosophist Central Shrine was in Bombay. The average Christian had a low enough opinion of theosophy before Madame Blavatsky appeared on the scene to found her own theosophical school in Madras in 1875. *Blunt's Dictionary of Sects*, published in 1874, refers to the theosophist's 'preposterous claims' and 'arrogant pretensions' and regrets that no uniform principle or system of belief can be described 'for in each period of their grotesque existence they listened submissively to the voice of their leaders, which rarely echoed reason'.

At no point does the Reverend John Henry Blunt attempt an appraisal of the aims of the early theosophists. He ignores the alchemical table of 'correspondences' – a system of figurative teaching by no means unrelated to his own Christian one. To him the 'gold' of the fire-philosophers was illusory and worthless.

The founding father of theosophy was Paracelsus, a Swiss doctor who lived from 1493 to 1541 – Erasmus and Frobenius were among his patients. Blunt acknowledges that Paracelsus was the 'discoverer' of opium and mercury, in being the first to put them to medical use, and is obviously puzzled that Paracelsus was a man of some stature. From an inability to understand that scientists could be deeply concerned with disciplines of spirit and the controlling mechanisms of mental states Blunt dismisses the subject that was to enthrall Jung:

> A man of prodigious vanity, he [Paracelsus] was glad to adopt the hyperbolical language of alchemy to magnify his discoveries, and partly perhaps to confuse his opponents, accustomed to the simple dialectic of the Aristotelian philosophy.

After noting the odd fact that after his death Paracelsus' followers were chemists and 'only secondarily prophets' Blunt gives short notices to the lives of Robert Fludd, the English disciple of Paracelsus who lived from 1574–1637, and Jacob Boehme, a convert of Fludd's who, Blunt tells us, 'set up a strange mystical system of his own'. These early theosophists were called Rosicrucians.

Eva read the works of Jacob Boehme and uses imagery in her poetry that combines the alchemical symbolism she absorbed from early theosophy, properly Rosicrucianism, with familiar

Christian metaphors from the New Testament. We most frequently come across the correspondence of Christ with the Cross
with Light (the alchemist used the cross as a symbol for light as it
incorporates all the letters of LVX) and of the rose with Mary the
mother of Christ – one of the names by which Mary was known
was 'Rosa Rosarum' and the symbol of the Rosicrucians was a
cross-marked heart at the centre of an open rose.

Blunt gave a more detailed account of the beliefs held by
Rosicrucians. He found that to them 'the only true knowledge
was to be derived by analysis of all bodies by the agency of fire',
and also 'that Good operated by the same laws in the Kingdom of
Grace as in the Kingdom of Nature and there is a complete
analogy and coincidence between science and religion' and the
last belief, carried on into the modern theosophy of the twentieth
century, was that a 'divine soul or energy is diffused through the
fabric of the universe – "the Universal Spirit".' Blunt notes that
part of the teachings of Rosicrucianism were conveyed in
astrology, magic and demonology.

One of the beliefs of modern theosophy that must have given
great comfort to Eva, who had regularly been visited by her
grandmother after her death, was that of 'astral forms' – a
phantasm of a person, living or dead, capable of separation and
distance from the flesh of the bodily form. The Society for
Psychical Research had catalogued hundreds of such cases in
their *Phantasms of the Living*, the first major survey published by
the Society. The resurrection of Christ presented no problem to
Eva. Her problems with Christianity arose from her failure to
understand the message. When she began to re-read the New
Testament she chose to concentrate on the Gospel of Saint John.

Eva treats this as an eye-witness account of Christ's life by his
favourite disciple (John was referred to as 'the beloved disciple')
written down at about AD 100. It is very different from the other
three Gospels; Matthew, Mark and Luke wrote their accounts
before John, and as these three are given roughly from the same
point of view they are called 'the Synoptic Gospels'. St John's
gospel is more complicated in attempting to fuse Jewish, Greek
and Gnostic ideas; it is more philosophical in its teaching and uses
metaphor to liken Christ to natural things such as bread, a vine,
or light.

Eva had studied Gnosticism – the first attempt to build a
philosophy of Christianity – that Blunt again deplores in his

Dictionary as 'a maze of incoherent absurdity'. It was a rigorous system of purification to bring the body 'into subjection to the spirit', to draw man from the world of moral darkness to moral light. Gnosticism interested Eva as there are many parallels between it and Buddhism, and as Blunt noted 'so much analogy . . . as to suggest some connection between them'.

We find all these strands woven into Eva's writings on the New Testament. In a talk given to the Hampstead Theosophical Society in November 1925, called 'Reincarnation and Transmutation in the New Testament', Eva remarks on Christ's use of Old Testament imagery, for example, his referring back to the Book of Jeremiah and the Psalms in his 'I am the true Vine' images, and of his insistence on washing his disciples' feet:

> It is interesting to note that many of the symbols used by Christ to express the inexpressible are in themselves very ancient, and would therefore be perhaps more easily understood two thousand years ago than now. Thus they would have little meaning for orthodox modern philosophy. But in astrology we find both water and feet used as psychic symbols, and fire, as in the New Testament, for spiritual love . . . . Astrology itself, however modernised, is inspired and dominated by very ancient Asiatic ideas: one often seems to see in it the remains of some prehistoric religion. Also I venture to suggest that the idea of the psychic in the New Testament corresponds in some ways to what many people are accustomed to call the Astral.

Evelyn Underhill, the distinguished writer on mysticism, had become a friend of Eva's in London and in her introduction to Eva's book of religious poems, *The House of Three Windows*, traces Eva's route through the '-isms':

> We see her innate sense of 'otherness' finding its first obvious affinities with the dreamy mysticality of Celtic poems and legends . . . we see her mind early disclosing the strongly Platonic bent which it retained throughout its growth . . . . We see the emergence of a spiritual outlook which might almost be called pantheistic, though influenced on the one hand by the Neoplatonists and on the other by that doctrine of reincarnation which never ceased to attract her. Especially strong in her at this stage was the consciousness of all that Plotinus

meant by *Psyche*: a sense of the indwelling Spirit that cherishes and gives unity to all life .... In her later work we see the transformation of this Platonic spirituality into lofty Christian mysticism . . .'

Eva was dead when Evelyn Underhill wrote her introduction – the volume of poems was published later in the year of her death. After paying tribute to the effectiveness and sincerity of Eva's poetry, she says farewell to her with a quotation: 'At the end of her Revelations, Julian of Norwich, the first and greatest of English women mystics, gathered all the strands of her many-coloured thought into the single phrase "Love was the meaning".'

The meaning of love in St John's Gospel was Eva's subject in her study, 'A psychological and poetic approach to the study of Christ in the Fourth Gospel' – a large book of 363 pages published by Longmans in 1923; and having understood its meaning, how to practise it, for, Eva wrote: 'To seek to enter into other people's lives without love is the fundamental mistake of all governing and judicial systems.'

Commenting on John XVII verses 20–3, 'that they all may be one . . .' and the keeping of the commandment to love one another, Eva writes:

> True Christian Love is something much more than goodwill, or even affection. Its mental side, the truth that is love, is what we call imagination. It is the power of projecting oneself into other people's lives so that one feels their sufferings as one's own. Where there is imagination there can be no cruelty or unkind-ness. It is not that the imaginative person thinks it wrong to make another suffer, it is that when another suffers he suffers himself. A soldier in times of war, with a little imagination, is a miserable being. A soldier, with a universal imagination, would not be able to kill another person of any nationality whatever
> . . .

Eva's name was attached to as many good causes as was Mrs Despard's. After the execution of Roger Casement she and Esther had found time for yet another in the League for the Abolition of Capital Punishment and as vegetarians and animal lovers their help was enlisted by anti-vivisectionists and the RSPCA. In 1925 an event called 'Animal Week' was organised and Eva went to Tunbridge Wells to speak to the Theosophical Society there on 'The Cry of the Dumb'. She told the story of Christ meeting a man who was beating a donkey that had fallen down under too heavy a load. Christ asked the man why he was beating the animal, as the load was too heavy and the donkey was in pain. The man answered that the animal was his, he had paid for it; the disciples, who knew the man, supported him. Christ asked them, 'Do you not see how she bleeds, and do you not hear how she laments and cries?' They could not; saddened, Christ said, 'Woe will come to those who hear not how she cries . . . .' He healed the donkey, but in pity said to the man: 'Go and smite no more thy beasts, that thou mayest not be thyself in misery.'

This is the story that Eva used to illustrate the extension of imaginative pity not only to humans but into the animal world:

> This story seems to hit at the root of all cruelty, direct or indirect. For there are many people who would not directly do a cruel action, and yet do not realize the terrible truth that a large proportion of human life, and specially human festivity, is founded on the sufferings of animals, nor feel in any way responsible for those sufferings. Sensitiveness to suffering outside ourselves is surely the greatest gift of Love . . . . We have all known people who put us to shame by the kindness of their everyday lives, and yet at the same time are capable of countenancing all sorts of cruelty in relation to animals, or even to weaker races of men. And this is not from any unkindness or cruelty of nature, but simply from want of imagination, a very specialised form of mental power. To hear the dumb things cry is not given to every man . . . people, especially children or savages, are often cruel, not from a wish to hurt, but from an incapacity to understand anything so unrelated to their own sensations as sensitiveness in the shadowy lives that surround them.

We see why Evelyn Underhill praised Eva's ability to express the spiritual simply and directly, describing her late Christian poems as 'concentrated, concrete and personal'. Through her concentration on the Gospel of St John, Eva came to an acute awareness of Christ, and in her poems realises him as a presence, as she does in *Christ in the Lane*:

This morning, through the gold and green,
Christ walked, by men unseen,
But the blue flower in the lane
Said as he passed, quite plain,
'Speed well, speed well, O Strange and True,
We have waited long for you.'
His robe in a bramble caught and frayed
Thorns shrank, by memories dismayed,
Till from his garment's tattered hem
Peace flowed on them.
To hold his Love was lifted up
The celandine's gold cup.
The small green fronds uncurling cried
'We thought you had died, we thought you had died.'
Like Mary's ointment, golden sweet
The gorse spilt fragrance at his feet.
Joyful and splendid the white May
Proclaimed the Resurrection Day.
O Christ, a burden of gloom
May haunt the wallèd room,
But the blue shining out of doors
   Is yours, is yours.

In order to study Christ's life thoroughly Eva went back to the fourth- and fifth-century Greek manuscripts of the Gospel in the British Museum. She checked her own translations against the many published versions of bible scholars. In the 'Suggestions and Interpretations' chapter in her book on the Fourth Gospel she writes of the difficulties of translation – particularly of the intrusion of gender into the spiritual sphere and the unnecessary confusion following, for example, the translation from the Greek of 'Word' as 'he' and of 'Light' as 'it'. She goes on:

It seems as if the English language left no room for the conception of Life transcending sex. For the pronoun conveying the idea of God, one is reduced to choosing between 'he' and 'she' both with rigid sex associations, or 'it' with its associations of sub-human or undeveloped human life, or what we call lifelessness ... but in Greek this difficulty does not arise. The arbitrary gender of nouns robs the 'he' or 'it' of any significance beyond that of grammar. Some authorities connect the expression 'logos' with the 'Sophia' of the wisdom books. It is curious to think that if the word Sophia (wisdom) had been used by John instead of 'Logos' the translators would have been logically obliged to put the whole into the feminine, 'In her was life' etc. If one first stipulates that the word 'it' shall mean the very essence of real life and no idea of lifelessness, the easiest way of avoiding the gender difficulty seems to be to give up the 'he's' and 'she's' and stick to the neuter.

The restricting, limiting constraints of gender were a life-long preoccupation and bane to Eva, who longed to throw the whole amateur theatrical performance of 'womanliness' and 'manliness' overboard. The close of her last paragraph above reminds us of Virginia Woolf, echoing Donne, longing to be 'beyond the hee and shee'.

At the close of St John's Gospel Christ, on the cross, gives John and his mother to each other, to be to each other what he was to both of them; the general manner of his love for women – that we see in his defence of the woman taken in adultery – led Eva to be very perplexed by the incident during the marriage in Cana where Mary says, 'They have no wine' and Christ answers with the strange words: 'Woman, what have I to do with thee? Mine hour is not yet come' (verse 4, Chapter 2). Following what should have been a severe put-down, Mary serenely tells the servants to do whatever her son tells them to do. Whatever Christ said it did not offend her. Westcott, in his *Gospel according to Saint John*, does acknowledge that the phrase is doubtful, but he keeps it, as it is the wording of the other three gospels.

Eva began to worry at the phrase suspecting that a local idiom or colloquialism had been mistranscribed. She broke down the Greek into either 'what . . . mine and thine' or 'what to me and to thee' and, working backwards from the fact that Mary reacted to Christ's remark in a positive way, she reasoned that the phrase was more likely to have meant something like 'what is mine is thine'.

Certainly Mary's appeal was instantly answered, an important point to Eva as the damning phrase, 'Woman, what have I to do with thee', is precious evidence from holy writ to the male supremacist. Eva argues her way onwards:

The fact that Christ called his mother 'woman' instead of 'mother', added to the seeming snub of 'what have I to do with thee?' has been a stumbling block to some people. But if the words really mean 'what is mine is thine, woman', the substitution of the impersonal word 'woman' for the personal 'mother' only implies the ignoring of a mere physical relation, in the face of real spiritual nearness. His mother, like any other woman or man, was his friend, to whom he would give all that he had. This point of view seems to rule out the attempt of some critics to prove some kind of nearer relation between Christ and his men disciples, than that which existed between him and his women disciples. Westcott remarks of the sentence that it shows Christ could not take a suggestion from a woman, even if that woman was his mother. This is an important point, because ideas like this must always tend to feed the subconscious vanity in persons of one sex, and the laziness in persons of the other . . . . In external things they are the deep subconscious justification in people's minds for the extraordinary exclusion of women from celebrating the Eucharist and preaching, an exclusion none the less materialistic and extraordinary because for many years unquestioned. In Christ there is neither male nor female . . .

Eva's criticism of the received translation of the Bible came quite late in the day, for women scholars of Greek and Hebrew had begun this assault in the middle of the nineteenth century. In America the publication of *The Woman's Bible* in 1895 caused a furore that split the woman's movement there. One of the revising committee that produced this woman's version of the Bible, Matilda Joslyn Gage, shocked conservative women to the core by addressing a prayer to 'God, our Mother' at the opening of a woman's rights conference.

The organiser of *The Woman's Bible*, Elizabeth Cady Stanton, thought that it was crucial for women to expurgate the Old and New Testaments as being unfit for use as they stood: 'Especially if we wish to inspire our children with proper love and respect for the Mothers of the Race.' Cady Stanton had studied Greek to please her father when his only son died. She also became an expert horsewoman, but to no avail. Her father could not be consoled, or value her as he had valued her brother. Very early in life she became aware that as men had always translated the Bible, their version was lop-sided, edited and translated in a man-identified way. She was eighty-three by the time that *The*

Woman's Bible was published, having hauled a very long haul against prevailing opinion. In her introduction she fires away at the contradictions she sees in male Christianity: 'Some churchmen speak of maternity as a disability, and then chant the Magnificat in all their cathedrals round the globe.'

The Woman's Bible used a translation by the American scholar Julia Smith that was published in 1876. Eva evidently had not heard of it or *The Woman's Bible* for they treat the episode at the marriage of Cana in a different way:

> There was no disrespect intended in the word 'woman' with which Jesus addressed his mother, as the greatest princesses were accosted thus by their servants in the same manner among the ancients. Jesus merely intended to suggest that no-one could command when he should perform miracles, as they would in any ordinary event subject to human discretion.

This makes Eva's case for the mistranslation of this particular passage seem far-fetched, but when we read the splendid commentary in *The Woman's Bible* fulminating against the texts so lowering to the status of women we see an exact correspondence between it and Eva's ideas in working to remove the taint of unclean animal status from women and to grant them full humanity.

As Eva wrote:

> Perhaps few besides women will appreciate the importance of the fact that women were not mothers or sisters to Christ, that he cared nothing for physical qualities and relationships. Women were to him simply human beings embarked, like all others, on the Divine adventure of life, that true Life where 'that which is without is as that which is within and the male with the female neither male nor female' (Traditional Sayings of Jesus: Clem. Rom., Epist., 11–12).

These ideas about the superficiality of gender were enlarged upon by the journal *Urania*, which although privately printed and not officially published or for sale, certainly circulated. Almost evangelical in tone it encouraged its readers to get on the right path and give up that bad habit called gender. Shortly after Eva and Esther moved to London a group of men and women interested in the reform of relations between the sexes came together, acknowledging Eva as 'our leader' – as she is referred to in editorials – and founded *Urania*.

Urania asked for the abandonment of traditional sex-roles, believing them completely artificial and dishonest, and tending to make a game or theatrical performance of male/female relations, and marriage a useless system where once one of the pair had tired of their part in the drama he or she could simply walk off-stage and audition for a part in another play. Many men in Eva's social circle recognised the theatricality of the female response to the male, without a second look at male behaviour. Horace Plunkett, for example, particularly relished a quatrain by 'Cynicus' addressed to Shakespeare:

> You wrote a line too much, my sage,
> Of seers the first, the first of sayers;
> For only half the world's a stage,
> And only all the women players.

By such mockery and by direct criticism clear-eyed men and women worried away at the age-old impulse of women conditioned to attach themselves to men as dependants. 'Cynicus' mocks, but Ada Nield Chew in an article 'Let the women be alive!' in the *Freewoman*, April 1912, is shatteringly direct: 'A woman who lives on a man's earnings, even though "respectably" married, is as much a prostitute as her outcast sister of the streets.'

Wishing to show women horizons beyond their reproductive systems, *Urania* deplored over-emphasis on women's childbearing capacities and, in attacking this, showed almost disgust for the change then taking place in women's behaviour in becoming more openly sexual, a type of sexual freedom in women's behaviour at this stage that was seen as a blind turning by *Urania*:

The emancipated modern girl interprets her freedom as freedom to enslave herself to men. It might almost be inferred that Freedom means nothing else. The acceptance of her biological destiny takes precedence of the fulfilment of her soul – to her utter degradation. The ideal woman of forty years ago was an ethereal creature, who disdained to be bound by the limitation of her body, although she might, through tradition, through vanity or through poverty, be brought into the possession of a lover. She was not a biological machine wallowing before every passable man. The 'frankness' and 'realism' and 'candour' of the present day spell, not freedom, but Enslavement of the Spirit, to a purgatory of physiology.

In the 1920s, *Urania* did have membership drives – the front cover might carry this arresting appeal:

There is a vista before us of a Spiritual progress which far transcends all political matters. It is the abolition of the 'manly' and the 'womanly'. Will you not help to sweep them into the museum of antiques? Don't you care for the union of all fine qualities in one splendid ideal?

The membership lists and subscription lists for *Urania* have not survived, so it is not known how large a number were attracted by these ideals. Eva herself appears to have written a manifesto for *Urania* – it has her ring of conviction and a quotation in Greek – but it is difficult to imagine the average woman of 1924 reading it and being anything but seriously alarmed since she is asked to throw away so much:

Urania denotes the company of those who are firmly determined to ignore the dual organisation of humanity in all its manifestations. They are convinced that this duality has resulted in the formation of two warped and imperfect types. They are further convinced that in order to get rid of this state of things no measures of 'emancipation' or 'equality' will suffice, which do not begin by a complete refusal to recognise or tolerate the duality itself. If the world is to see sweetness and independence combined in the same individual, all recognition of that duality must be given up. For it inevitably brings in its train the suggestion of the conventional distortions of character which are based on it. There are no 'men' or 'women' in Urania. 'All' eisin hôs angeloi.' [But they are like angels.]

The angelic state of release from the body was by this time one that Eva longed for. Her cancer of the bowel began to spread at about Christmas time of 1924 – it took eighteen months to kill her. As food could not pass the internal obstruction Eva began to eat less and less, and she became dehydrated. What little she did eat or drink caused vomiting. Yeats apparently saw her at this stage 'withered and skeleton gaunt' and not realising that he was looking at a case of intestinal cancer went on to immortalise her in this condition as 'an image of such politics'.

CHAPTER 10

WORLD WAR ONE: PEACE AND RETIREMENT

Non-violent resistance was a well-developed aspect of the Eastern beliefs that interested theosophists like Eva. Both Eva and Esther referred to themselves as 'extreme pacifists' and when the editor of *Urania* printed a short obituary notice for Esther its most prominent feature was: 'Extremely averse from all violence, she once declared in our hearing that she "would not shoot a pursuing tiger!" Such uncompromising *ahisma* is surely the root of all real progress.'

Unfortunately the majority remained unenlightened and it can only have been with horror that Eva and Esther saw Emmeline and Christabel Pankhurst become the tools of Lloyd George and turn into jingoistic recruiting officers in fine ladies' clothes. In the absence of the men at war women came to do all those skilled jobs previously thought beyond their competence and Eva and Esther saw the sudden opening up of trades and professions into which they had been trying to push the thin edge of the wedge for so many years. But this triumph was of no interest to them in the face of such a war.

The NUWSS split over whether to support militarism or to advocate peace, and after a dreadful and long-drawn-out confrontation with Mrs Fawcett who was a diehard Britisher, Catherine Marshall, Helena Swanwick, Chrystal Macmillan and others seceded and formed a British peace movement. The Women's International Congress at The Hague in 1915 was to be a brave effort. Esther and Eva were both members of the British organising committee and on this committee we find massed long-serving unionist and suffragist women and many impressive names like Sylvia Pankhurst, Emily Hobhouse (with whom Eva had worked on the anti-Boer war protest), Lilian Harris, from the Women's Co-operative Guild, Mrs Despard, Margaret Bondfield of the Shop Assistants Union and the Adult Suffrage Society, Margaret Llewelyn Davies, Katherine Glasier and Ethel Snowden from the ILP, and old friends Sarahs Reddish and Dickenson.

The peace women composed a letter to their German sisters:

'On Earth Peace, Goodwill toward Men'

To the WOMEN OF GERMANY & AUSTRIA
OPEN CHRISTMAS LETTER

Sisters,

Some of us wish to send you a word at this sad Christmastide though we can but speak through the press. The Christmas message sounds like mockery to a world at war, but those of us who wished and still wish for peace may surely offer a solemn greeting to such of you who feel as we do. Do not let us forget that our very anguish unites us, that we are passing together through the same experiences of pain and grief.

Caught in the grip of terrible Circumstance, what can we do? Tossed on this turbulent sea of human conflict, we can but moor ourselves to those calm shores whereon stand, like rocks, the eternal verities – Love, Peace, Brotherhood.

We pray you to believe that come what may we hold to our faith in Peace and Goodwill between nations; while technically at enmity in obedience to our rulers, we own allegiance to that higher law which bids us live at peace with all men.

Though our sons are sent to slay each other, and our hearts are torn by the cruelty of this fate, yet through pain supreme we will be true to our common womanhood. We will let no bitterness enter into this tragedy, made sacred by the life-blood of our best, nor mar with hate the heroism of their sacrifice. Though much has been done on all sides you will, as deeply as ourselves, deplore, shall we not steadily refuse to give credence to those false tales so freely told us, each of the other?

We hope it may lessen your anxiety to learn we are doing our utmost to soften the lot of your civilians and war prisoners within our shores, even as we rely on your goodness of heart to do the same for ours in Germany and Austria.

Do you not feel with us that the vast slaughter in our opposing armies is a stain on civilisation and Christianity, and that still deeper horror is aroused at the thought of those innocent victims, the countless women, children, babes, old and sick, pursued by famine, disease and death in the devastated areas, both East and West?

As we saw in South Africa and the Balkan States, the brunt of modern war falls upon non-combatants, and the conscience of the world cannot bear the sight.

Is it not our mission to preserve life? Do not humanity and commonsense alike prompt us to join hands with the women of neutral countries, and urge our rulers to stay further bloodshed?

Relief, however colossal, can reach but few. Can we sit still and let the helpless die in their thousands, as die they must – *unless* we rouse ourselves in the name of Humanity to save them? There is but one way to do this. We must all urge that peace be made with appeal to Wisdom and Reason. Since in the last resort it is these which must decide the issues, can they begin too soon, if it is to save the womanhood and childhood as well as the manhood of Europe?

Even through the clash of arms we treasure our poet's vision, and already seem to hear

'A hundred nations swear that there shall be

Pity and Peace and Love among the good and free.'

May Christmas hasten that day. Peace on Earth is gone, but by renewal of our faith that it still reigns at the heart of things, Christmas should strengthen both you and us and all womanhood to strive for its return.

We are yours in this sisterhood of sorrow . . .

War-mongering, of the kind that Emmeline and Christabel Pankhurst went in for, and the disastrous death tolls, quickly established a public mood of intense patriotism and the compassionate impulse of most women to support their 'menfolk' was immediate and unthinking. The highly-skilled and dangerous work done by women during the war in the armament and munitions factories and in auxiliary and nursing service at the

Front was probably the greatest factor in the granting of the vote to women at the end of the war.

The anti-German feeling was acute, and detestation of the peace women and conscientious objectors knew no bounds. They were shamefully and violently treated. Helena Swanwick, sister of the painter Walter Sickert and prominent in the British peace movement, was half Danish, half English but perfectly Germanic-looking, and her sufferings (there was a press campaign against her as a German agent) were typical of the conviction at this time that peace people were either mad, spineless cranks or dangerous infiltrators in the pay of Germany who aimed to ruin the war effort by substituting pacifism for patriotism. The history of the support system run by the seceding pacifist members of the NUWSS for conscientious objectors and their families is still to be thoroughly reclaimed by the historians of the peace movement.

Eva Gore-Booth in her pacifist plays returns often to the old stumbling-block of 'manliness' and its associations with might and the exercise of power. In her *Deirdre*, Naosi asks in horror, when Deirdre asks him to put aside his weapons: 'Do you want me a woman?' and this takes us back to the old arguments of the anti-suffragists of the 1890s: not to be a man is to be an 'incompetent', which by World War One had extended to 'incompetent and non-combatant'. Society's revenge on the conscientious objectors shows us exactly how this syndrome worked. After the war, conscientious objectors were forbidden to vote – disenfranchised – for five years whereas the women who had become more 'manly' by war service – showing their technical competence, nerve and stamina – were enfranchised.

So that although the male image of women was opened to change, the change was for women to become more like men – there was no tendency for men to accept any 'womanly' characteristics as desirable. Prophets like Edward Carpenter were crying in the wilderness when they asked for men to unlearn their traditional forceful role.

With the prevailing public mood it was practically impossible to justify moral revulsion at the use of force, and conscientious objectors were simply thought of as cowards – perhaps the increasing understanding of modern peace movement ideals will lead to an open acknowledgement of their integrity and bravery.

The wives and children of conscientious objectors were 'sent to Coventry' and cut dead by their neighbours. In Manchester, a woman who was influenced by Eva Gore-Booth, Constance Andrews, set up a school and church that helped such families. This was to be a familiar line for pacifist suffragists during the war. Selina Cooper did similar welfare work with mothers and children.

Constance Andrews was a pacifist, a theosophist and a Minister. Her ministry is described in articles in *Urania*. She herself officiated at the Church of the New Age and she had a licence to perform marriages. Her ministry and work in Manchester were reported with approval in *Urania* and it is not surprising to find Uranian ideas on sexuality in her publications, like *New Age Teachings*. She reasoned that only the false male conviction of the natural subservience of women had barred women from priesthood and ministry and that to demonstrate the female capacity for ministry, as she ably did herself, would open the way to an equality between men and women in spiritual as well as daily life:

I.

¶*The Church of the New Age admits men and women to its Ministry and membership on terms of perfect equality.*

THE SECRET OF SEX.

The greatest test of qualification for the Ministry is Purity of Life and this quality is associated with true womanhood as well as with true manhood.

A true Priesthood is independent of and above sex, when it has the knowledge of the inner meaning taught by Christ, who, in speaking to His Disciples on this subject, said, "All men cannot receive this saying, save they to whom it is given. He that is able to receive it, let him receive it." He who receives it is of the Priesthood and needs no intermediary between himself and the Christ within. Christ re-iterated the mystic universal truth of all ages—The Kingdom of Heaven is within you.

If the real meaning of sex were understood and appreciated, men and women would be able to develop the higher part of their nature. It is because in sex there lies a wonderful meaning, that it has become the most thought of thing in the world. It is because the thought in regard to sex has become impure and unreal, that women have been debarred from the Priesthood. In religion the thought in regard to sex has been materialised. In other departments of life romance has crept in and sublimated the link between man and woman. But most forms of religion have led to the degradation of women. For the truth that men and women are made in the Image of God, has been substituted the false idea that man was made in the Image of God, and that woman was created to fulfil the will of man by bearing him children after the law of the flesh. What was not, and is not understood, is that both men and women have the power, not only of physical generation, but of spiritual creation. They possess the creative powers of thought, of imagination and will. These powers are independent of the sex of the body, for they are soul powers. The soul is in possession of these, whether it works through the body of a man or a woman.

Studying the various forms of religion throughout the times recorded by history, we find that the creative power of the Soul has been vaguely understood but it has been grossly misapplied.

Woman has been looked upon as the divine representative of the soul, but men have worshipped, not the soul, but the body. The bodies of women have been sacrificed because of the vain and foolish idea that the sensual body represents the spiritual soul. This idea led to the criminal sacrifice of women in the Temples and to the prostitution of their bodies, in the imaginary hope that such sacrifice would be acceptable to God.

But a New Age is dawning when men and women can stand together as human beings possessed of divine souls.

When St. Paul used his intuition, and thus brought forth the soul knowledge within him, he said, "There is neither Jew nor Greek, there is neither bond nor free, there is neither male nor female; for ye are all one in Christ Jesus."

Two ex-pupils of the School of the New Age and who had attended services regularly at the Church of the New Age replied to an appeal for information in the *Manchester Evening News* in November 1986. Mrs G. M. Leggatt wrote:

> First I must tell you how we came to go to 'The New Thought School'. My father was interned in the first World War and it was the kindness of Mrs Neish who through the church helped Mum. Mrs Neish's daughter May was the secretary and consequently we three children were sent to the Sunday School, it was after May 1915 . . . . The Church comprised a suite of offices at 19, Brazenose St. in the centre of Manchester, it consisted of the Reception Hall, the Church Hall, the Healing Room and Library and Kitchen . . . . The Church Hall had seating for 150–200, no more, and consequently the Memorial Hall in Albert Square was hired for Sunday evenings and various other things – parties and American teas (the whole Church developed in America, the head being Mrs Klaus) . . . . The main theme of all services was peace and love, with a very strong emphasis on re-incarnation, over the doorways was 'Know thyself' and 'To thine own self be true.' The original church has now been demolished and new offices built . . . .
>
> Each week there was a five minutes silence for concentration on Peace, Love and Health. Names of sick people were read out . . . also most were vegetarians.

This shows a familiar clustering in the suffragist world of feminism, pacifism, vegetarianism and a working-class base. The touchstone for this type would be Mrs Despard who in 1916 and 1917 was on the councils of: the Women's Freedom League, the Women's International League, the No-Conscription Fellowship, the National Campaign for Civil Liberties, the Theosophical Society, the London Vegetarian Society, the Battersea Labour Party, the Women's Labour League, the Home Rule for India Committee and the Women's Peace Crusade.

The Peace Crusade and the Women's International League for Peace both used the colour blue in their symbolism and it is interesting that in Mrs Leggatt's sketch groundplan of the Church Rooms in Brasenose Street 'The Healing Room' has the note: 'all in Blue various shades (Peace)'.

National Service for single males was introduced by the government in January 1916. The Independent Labour Party had a long tradition of international co-operation and it was not surprising that the men and women who first felt compelled to state their pacifism and objection to conscriptions were ILP members. The No-Conscription Fellowship (NCF) had been founded early in 1915 by Fenner Brockway and Clifford Allen with Catherine Marshall, prominent NUWSS organiser and Parliamentary Secretary for that union until 1915. Marshall had a pronounced talent for conversion and had roped in the invaluable Bertrand Russell by mid-1916.

From the beginning the NCF was heavily swayed by women – the fellowship had been the brainchild of Fenner Brockway's wife Lilla – and we find many prominent suffragists like Eva and Esther involved in its organisation. A great deal was asked of this organisation; by the Military Service Act, conscripting all men between the ages of 18 and 41, a tribunal system was set up to examine the individual case of each conscientious objector.

Eva and Esther's chief work for the NCF consisted of travelling to these tribunal courts all over the country to speak in defence of conscientious objectors (COs) and to give personal support to each man as his case came up.

A feature of women's campaigns, from whichever segment of the political spectrum they issued, was a distinct flair for publicity through spectacle and grand proportions. Theatricals, parades, bazaars, 'monster' meetings were staged effectively; women had some experience of using these aids in the cause of suffragism and in 1917 they came to use them for peace. The Women's Peace Crusade was the creation of Agnes Dollan and Helen Crawford, both socialists living in Glasgow. The Crusade had massive support on Clydeside. By midsummer their open-air meetings had created such interest and support that over 12,000 people gathered for a huge demonstration in Central Glasgow on 8 July. Agnes Dollan and Helen Crawford, Ethel Snowden and Helena Swanwick, were the main speakers.

Manchester, inspired by Glasgow's example, started its own campaign, but in the English North and Midlands there was mass hostility to the Peace Crusade and police protection was needed for the procession of women with their 'peace' banners. The 'peace women', as they were called, put on plays and distributed literature to inform the general public on pacifism as a possible moral choice. Eva Gore-Booth's propaganda writings like the *Tribunal* and her Irish plays were probably written for the 'peace women'.

Eva had long been fascinated by the story of Maeve; from childhood she had known the extraordinary burial mound on Knocknarea, supposed to be Maeve's, that is visible from many of the windows of Lissadell. She first attempted to write on Maeve in 1902 in a play called the *Triumph of Maeve*. In her preface to this play we see why Eva's obsession with the Irish warrior-queen was to intensify during the years of World War One; she wrote:

> The story of Maeve stands to me as a symbol of the world-old struggle in the human mind between the forces of dominance and pity, of peace and war. The reign of the old warlike gods is rashly broken into and threatened by the fascination of a new idea. The birth of imagination, the new god of pity, is symbolised in the outside world by the crucifixion of Christ. A vision of this event is seen by Maeve at the moment of its happening, and becomes the turning point in her life and thought . . . . But Fionavar, her great joy in life, goes down to meet her mother returning in triumph from the fight, suddenly sees the death and pain of the battlefield, and falls dead, crying in bitterness 'Is this the triumph of Maeve?'

Developing the ideas of the *Triumph of Maeve*, Eva began work on a thoroughly pacifist protest-play called *The Buried Life of Deirdre* in 1908 and then laid it aside. In the winter of 1916–17 she became very ill through exhaustion brought on by overwork – she was travelling extensively through 1916 for both the No-Conscription Fellowship and in efforts to aid her imprisoned sister. In her sick-bed she began a revision of *Deirdre* and made a series of illustrative drawings that are heavily influenced by the work of William Blake.

It is clear that by re-organising *The Buried Life of Deirdre*, Eva was setting her mind to rights, calming herself with remembrance and recognising with gratitude the good she had drawn from relationships. It was evidently important to her equilibrium, to restore her balance that was beset by the inhumanities of the world war on one hand and on the other the appalling events in Ireland where Constance revelled in the role of a latter-day Maeve. Eva sent Constance her work and it is not fanciful to speculate that the *Deirdre* play may be a special appeal to Constance.

The play may seem very stilted and formal in style but is quite typical of the Abbey Irish plays of the Celtic revival; the peculiar interest of Gore-Booth's *Deirdre* is that it shows the style surviving strongly until so late a date that we are able to read a pacifist reaction to World War One in a play with a cast list from ancient Irish myth – a type of play that as a rule until then had propagandised the cause of Irish nationalism and the struggle against England.

After the war Eva's health deteriorated and the year 1920–21 was spent in a slow wander about Italy. On their return Eva and Esther settled into their Hampstead house at 14 Frognal Gardens and Eva began her study of the Fourth Gospel. They kept open house, but Eva had ceased to do battle in the outside world. Esther was still an active campaigner, but from their return from Italy onwards, she gave much of her time to tending Eva.

Reginald Roper had shared houses with Esther and Eva at various periods during his life, from the time that he was a student at Owens College, and Eva came to live in the Roper house at Heald Place up to her last illness in Hampstead. He was an intimate of both women, and a very trusted familiar. He alone knew what his sister knew, that from Eva's 'dangerous illness' in 1925 she was dying of cancer of the bowel. Friends and relations had no inkling of what the Ropers concealed. It was especially kept from Constance, who was actually misled as to her sister's health. Official accounts state that she died 'after a brief illness' and her death was a sudden, most unexpected shock to Constance, who never recovered.

It seemed that in the last eighteen months of Eva's life the Ropers had a shift-system for night nursing and Reginald was present at Eva's death. It was he who witnessed the death certificate. Relief from pain, and short periods of sleep, came from morphine. Esther and Reginald were excellent nurses. Reginald had trained as a masseur and massage also gave Eva some ease. She moved entirely into the world of books and music. She re-read Greek texts and early mystics. She thought back to her start on Greek at Lissadell, and she still had her Lexicon:

> This Phaedo that I work on, glad, but weary eyed,
> (as ever and again,
> With care and pain,
> I search the heavy word book at my side)

> I read such years ago on summer eves
> . . . . Held by new magic in the translated page . . . .
> This strange delightful labour of my age
> Was my youth's wild and rainbow-lit romance.

She almost died at Christmas 1925 but rallied. The poem *New Year* (1926), beginning 'I have come forth from dark distress' and ending 'I am alive, alive, alive, High tide and sunrise in my mind', celebrates her escape. Esther sought out companions for her, to read aloud or play music, but on many days Eva literally sank into darkness, her vision no longer clear. She wrote in *Three Consolations in Illness*, her last long poem:

> A human hand outstretched reached down into the
> dark,
> I knew a friend was watching by my side
> Holding in her strong heart through the long night
> As in a lamp that dark and hidden light . . .

This was Esther, and towards the end a pianist friend played from *Parsifal* and this also reached her:

> The clouds came down amid a storm of pain
> There was no word from heaven,
> no word, no word,
> Then a friend came
> and played this music . . .

She gathered herself for one last affirmation:

> Yes, God is good, from his great heart there flows
> Hands to relieve, and gentle souls of friends;
> O wonderful friends, your patient deeds and kind
> Are the bright petals of the Mystic rose
> That grows where the world ends,
> The tree of life a-glitter in the wind.

At the age of fifty-six, Eva was physically almost worn away; she wrote one short poem in her last respite before death:

AFTER THE STORM

Suddenly everywhere
Clouds and waves are one,
The storm has cleared the air,
The sea holds the sun
And the blue sky –
There is no under, no above,
All is light, all is love –
Is it like this when you die?

A few weeks before she died Eva had been lying in pain on a couch in the garden at 14 Frognal Gardens when she had an ecstatic vision that flooded her with relief and peacefulness. She walked into the house to tell Esther what had happened.

Through the dedicatory speech that Esther made when she gave a memorial window to the University Settlement's Round House and through her Introduction to *The Complete Poems of Eva Gore-Booth* we actually know the very first and the very last words that Eva and Esther exchanged, and we know, too, that in a personal sense words were things that failed Esther:

Eva Gore-Booth's sensitive and loving nature made her a perfect friend. No words of mine could ever tell the beauty of her friendship, but I can say of it truly, 'Love never faileth.' Through years of difficult and trying work which we did together for thirty years she brought a spirit of adventure and gaiety which nothing daunted. Of a gallant courage and a gentle courtesy she made life together a gracious thing.

Formality was Esther's refuge and strength; if words failed her we can only try to understand her through her reaction to Eva's last vision and her part at her deathbed. When Eva came in from the garden she told Esther:

You know, I have always been afraid of death, and I could not get away from the fear of it. Then quite suddenly I heard the words, 'I will come to you' – slowly and clearly like that. I was almost stunned by the suddenness, and in my amazement and wonder could hardly believe for a moment. Then came the words 'I have promised – remember,' very distinctly. It was overwhelming. There was a radiance all around and I was filled with an extraordinary feeling of joy, the greatest I have ever known. 'Remember', she repeated twice emphatically, 'I shall never be afraid of death again.'

Esther continued:

Death came suddenly, after two days of illness, on 30 June 1926. She suffered terribly the last night, and suddenly said to me: 'This is death.' 'Yes it is', I said, 'but you told me you would never be afraid of it again.' 'Oh, no', she replied, 'I am not afraid, pray that it comes quickly.' At the end she looked up with that exquisite smile that always lighted up her face when she saw one she loved, then closed her eyes and was at peace.

July 9, 1926.

IN MEMORIAM.

EVA GORE-BOOTH

The death, after a short illness, of Eva Gore-Booth takes from us one of the most distinguished Christian poets of our time: a true mystic, whose work was the outcome not merely of "spiritual appreciation," but of profound spiritual experience. The career of Miss Gore-Booth, whose fragile physique only enhanced the impression of vivid inward life which was radiated by her whole personality, was a complete answer to those who regard the mystic as a person who remains aloof from the interests, struggles and sorrows of practical life. There was hardly any aspect of human existence which her passionate sense of spiritual reality did not make the more dear to her. She loved the poor, and was especially concerned to uphold the rights of working women and improve their economic position. During her early life in Manchester she was instrumental in forming the first of the women's trade unions; she championed the cause of the barmaids, when it was proposed to safeguard their morals by throwing them out of employment; and later succeeded in defeating an attempt to abolish the flower-girls' pitches in the London streets. She hated war, cruelty, greed, injustice, not merely for their own sakes, but because they conflicted with that eternal mercy and love which she felt to be the greatest of all realities. Alongside these practical and social sympathies ran that keen delight in art and in simple natural beauty which her poems reflect, the gift for friendship to which many can bear witness, and, especially in her later years, an alert and critical interest in the speculative side of religion. All these were various paths along which she pursued the eager and untiring search for perfection—that "life much more real and intense than this," for which alone she valued outer things.

> I have sought the Hidden Beauty in all things,
> In love, and courage, and a high heart, and a hero's
>   grave,
> In the hope of a dreaming soul, and a seagull's wings,
> In twilight over the sea, and a broken Atlantic wave,
> I have sought the Hidden Beauty in all things.

It is, however, as a mystical poet that Eva Gore-Booth will chiefly be remembered: and it is in her poems—especially the three volumes called *The One and the Many*, *The Agate Lamp*, and *The Shepherd of Eternity*—that her spiritual evolution can most clearly be traced. Like so many mystics, she was in her first period mainly theistic, even Neo-platonic, in outlook; afterwards developing the lofty Christocentric mysticism which inspired *The Shepherd of Eternity*, and her prose study of *Christ in the Fourth Gospel*. This strange arresting book contains an account, impressive in its humble directness and simplicity, of the personal experience which marked her entrance into the Christian mystical life—when her "eyes were suddenly and amazingly opened to the strange inner world."

"I could never doubt," she said, "the reality of the knowledge that, for years afterwards, seemed always unfolding itself from the same centre. Nor did I ever after feel that I did not know what Christ is really like. I tell this story, not because I want to claim any 'supernatural' authority for my thoughts . . . I record this experience because I must witness to the extraordinary mercy of Christ in taking the blindness from the eyes of a person in great need . . . and, though it is impossible to convey to others any sense of its vivid reality, my conviction of its truth has only grown more and more unshakable and compelling with the passing years."

Here we surely recognise that note of intense certitude which distinguishes the utterances of the real mystic from those of the mystical writer; and which places the poems of Eva Gore-Booth among those of that small group of poets who have not only sought, but have "found the Hiddden Beauty where the river finds the sea."

E.U.

(Eva's obituary for *The Times* was written by Evelyn Underhill.)

AFTERWORD

One of the very few personal letters of Esther's to survive was writen to Casimir Markievicz on the death of Constance in the year after Eva's death. Esther had been with Constance after her second operation for appendicitis. Constance was attended in hospital by Esther, the historian Dorothy MacArdle and Hannah Sheehy Skeffington, and it was these three who decided to telegram to Casimir to come from Warsaw, so that he and his son were with Constance when she died. There had been a great improvement in Constance's condition and Esther had returned to London on urgent business thinking that Constance was recovering. She was not. Casimir's telegram reached Esther almost as soon as she got in to Frognal Gardens. She replied:

My dear Casi and Stasko

I am quite crushed by the sudden end of our hopes. I would very much like to know whether anyone was with her – and if it was as sudden as it seems. Unless it will make any difference to any of her friends I think I shall not come back – but if you think it would – telegraph to me and I will come. I am so very thankful that you came. You gave Con such great pleasure. She loved having you. Please let me know what day you return here. I have arranged with Mordaunt that Casi shall be there and Stasko here as long as you like. Please let me know that is all

Yours ever, Esther.

Casimir did send for Esther, and both she and Reginald attended Constance's extraordinary public funeral through

Dublin to the 'peace of the Republican plot' at Glasnevin that Constance had longed for. There was a curious bond between Casimir and Esther who must have been looked upon by the Gore-Booths as mavericks who had taken Constance and Eva away from the family to strange lives given to politics and the working classes. Casimir stayed with Esther on the way back to Warsaw. He sat and read Constance's love letters. Esther was careful to stress the undying affection between Casimir and Constance when she gave an account of their marriage in *The Prison Letters of Countess Markievicz*. Wild rumours in Dublin had greatly offended both Casimir and Esther, and Esther was careful to correct these wherever and whenever she could.

After Eva's death Esther did not cease to work for the organisations to which Eva and Esther together had given all their energies. Indeed she added to her activities by preparing for the press both Eva's and Constance's manuscripts; she took to heart the last stanza of Eva's dedication to *The Buried Life of Deirdre*:

> You whose love's music to the inmost shrine
> Of Art can bear the feeblest words of life
> With chords and discords, splendour and great strife
> Make beautiful these feeble words of mine.

The Buried Life of Deirdre was produced very handsomely by Longmans in 1930, but Esther also gave a great deal of time to *The Complete Poems of Eva Gore-Booth* (1929) and the *Prison Letters of Countess Markievicz* (1934). During their years in Hampstead, Eva and Esther had often been guest speakers at Helen Neild's school, Pinehurst, and very soon after Eva's death we find Esther teaching history at the school. During the year 1927–8 in the class lists we find: 'European History with Miss Roper. 1815–Present Day'. Esther was at this stage already unhealthy – we never hear of her health when she was caring for the invalid Eva – and Miss Neild comments in her prefatory letter to the *Pinehurst Newsheet* on 26 April 1928: 'I must not close without a word of great thankfulness that we still have Miss Roper. Influenza caught her and she very nearly slipped away from us and is still only frail. I want to say much more, but she might read it, and you know how she takes revenge in her lectures? . . .'

Helen Neild had been a fellow student of Esther's at Owens;

another link with early Manchester days was Beatrice Collins who came to Pinehurst to give 'lantern lectures' on Italian cities. Eva had been very fond of her. A volume of Swinburne poems that she inscribed was given to Beatrice in Manchester in 1902. Twenty-five years later Beatrice, with Esther's brother Reginald, was to tend Esther in her last illness. Esther left her money to these two familiars.

Esther made her will in October 1927 choosing as her executors Reginald Roper and Beatrice Collins. T. P. Conwil Evans was appointed to succeed Esther as literary executor for Eva Gore-Booth at Esther's death. The witnesses to her will give final heartening evidence of the strength and longevity of pairing relationships between women in the suffrage movement. Here we find Katherine Rowton and Jane Lees now retired and living together at 31 Wolseley Road, Farncombe, Godalming, Surrey. They had worked with NESWS from the 1900 petition; Katherine Rowton took a prominent part in the formation of the National Industrial and Professional Women's Society in 1905 and was a long-serving close colleague of both Esther's and Eva's. Both Jane Lees and Katherine Rowton survived Esther. Her death certificate supplies an item of information that may explain Esther's reputation as a poor public speaker; her doctor, Dr Stuart-Harris, entered the cause of death as (1) Acute myocardial failure, and (2) Acute asthma. She appears to have spoken in short, staccato statements, so that asthma may have been the illness from which she was suffering when she was sent to Italy to recuperate in 1896. Eva may also have suffered from asthma as more than one description of her mentions that in speaking or reciting she gasped for breath.

On the surface Esther in the last decade of her life seemed calm and cheerful. Only some poems typed on loose sheets, and inserted into an Italian sketchbook of Eva's, indicate her hidden pain.

There is Verlaine's poem beginning 'O mon Dieu, vous m'avez blessé d'amour . . .', James Stephen's strange and ghastly poem 'The Fulness of Time' where Satan returns to 'his father and his friend' for 'Now the work is done / Enmity is at an end . . . And they seated him beside One who had been crucified!' There are two of Rainer Maria Rilke's poems – *Herbst* and *Vorgefuhl* – and the last is an extract from John Galsworthy's *Valley of the Shadow*:

God! I am travelling out to death's sea
I, who exulted in sunshine and laughter,
Dreamed not of dying . . .
    death is such a waste of me . . . . .
Grant me one prayer: Doom not the hereafter
Of mankind to war . . .
. . . Let not my sinking
in dark be for naught, my death a vain thing!
God, let me know it the end of man's fever!
Make my last breath a bugle call, carrying
Peace o'er the valleys and cold hills forever!

Esther did not survive the winter weather of 1937–8. She died at the end of April at the age of sixty-nine. She left her affairs in meticulous order; her death notices in *The Times* and *The Manchester Guardian* gave:

Roper – On April 28, at 14 Frognal Gardens, Hamstead, London, after a short illness, peacefully in her sleep, ESTHER GERTRUDE ROPER. Funeral at Hampstead Parish Church on Saturday April 30, at 12.15 p.m. Friends leave the house at twelve noon.

Eleven years before, in the year of Constance's death, Esther and Constance together had arranged that Esther and Eva should be buried in the same grave. The tombstone was inscribed with Eva's birth and death dates and a panel left for the addition of Esther's. Unlike Eva, Esther did not rate a *Times* obituary, and it requires long and thorough searching to discover any obituary notice at all.

The Manchester Guardian of 29 April 1938, in a general notice of London news headed 'Our London Correspondent', tucks in a short obituary at the end of a series of items of general interest:

The death of Miss Esther Roper adds another name to the long roll of women whose life was spent in the service of others . . . she stood for the practical application of the theory of liberty, equality and fraternity which is but another expression of the Christian faith.

From her early days as a student and graduate of Victoria University to the last weeks of her life her energies were devoted to the cause of peace and international friendship. To her many friends and to that wider circle of men and women who shared her long endeavour she will remain an example and an inspiration. (Anon.)

Esther's only true obituary appeared in *The Woman Teacher* on Friday, 20 May 1938. This was the journal of the National Union of Women Teachers that Esther had helped to found in 1919. It was written by a young teacher who had come to know Esther at the end of her life, Anne Prothero Jones:

The announcement in *The Times* of April 29th of the death of Miss Esther Roper will have come as a shock to many of her friends in the teaching world. Some of the older ones will remember past days wherein she formed one of a little group of plotters building schemes for the future which have material-ised in just such concrete form as, for instance, the NUWT. Younger people will remember the unfailing interest in them-selves and their profession, and her open-handed hospitality, for she always retained a particular fondness for those who taught and guided the up-coming generation.

As a young woman in the early days of the suffrage move-ment, Miss Roper took over the secretaryship of the Lancashire and Cheshire Women's Suffrage Society and later helped her friend Eva Gore-Booth with the campaign which supported the first women's suffrage candidate, at Wigan. Widely experi-enced among many classes of industrial women workers and a keen equalitarian ready and able to help all whom she con-sidered to be under the threat of injustice, her work will be sorely missed from societies such as The Open Door Council, of which she was an officer, which seeks to secure the equal treatment of men and women in industry and thus to remove a field of exploitation. Further, she worked for the abolition of the death penalty, and most faithfully, for peace based on international friendship.

But to those who knew the woman, Esther Roper herself remained the chief product of her remarkable life. Unselfish-ness, devotion, dogged patience do not often go hand-in-hand with a lively humour (and good humour), a penetrating insight into persons and affairs, and a steady tolerance of ideas and doctrines not her own. Frail of body, a rock-like sanity gave her a strength beyond the physical and those who visited her, even in illness, came away refreshed from contact with an unclouded spirit.

NOTES AND REFERENCES

Chapter 1 The Background and Childhood of Eva Gore-Booth

There are two main sources for the early life of Eva Gore-Booth, both compiled by Esther Roper: *Poems of Eva Gore-Booth*, the complete edition with *The Inner Life of a Child* and *Letters* and a biographical introduction of 48 pages, published by Longmans in 1929. More material relating to Eva was included in *Prison Letters of Countess Markievicz*, Longmans 1934, in the form of poems and articles by Eva on Easter Week in Dublin 1916, and further reminiscences by Esther about both sisters in her biographical sketch of 123 pages. No personal papers survive, manuscript poems and miscellaneous papers belonging to Eva were returned to the Gore-Booth family by Esther, and these survive.

A collection of books belonging to Eva and Esther was offered up for sale in Bristol in 1986 by an anonymous vendor; these supplied some dates and names of friends.

The best book to date on Constance Markievicz is *Constance de Markievicz. In the Cause of Ireland* by Jacqueline van Voris, The University of Massachusetts Press 1967. For those at sea in the subject of Irish politics in the nineteenth century a good short introduction is *Landlord or Tenant?* by Magnus Magnusson, Bodley Head 1978; more detailed is *Ireland Since the Famine* by F. S. L. Lyons, Fontana 1973.

Chapter 2 The Background and Childhood of Esther Roper

The *Church Missionary Gleaner* carried a long appreciation and death notice for Rev. Edward Roper in April 1877. The Rev. J. MacCartie published *Christian Assurance. Does it rest on Feeling or Faith?* by Edward Roper, with a memoir of Roper in a preface, in the same year.

The Church Missionary Society published Roper's *Facts about Foreign Missions in West Africa* in four tracts in 1868. Details of Edward Roper's career as a missionary are in *Register of Missionaries and Native Clergy*, CMS 1804–1904 (Part 1). Details on schooling and salaries, and the letter books of foreign missionaries, were found in the CMS Archive which has now been transferred to the Special Collections of Birmingham University Library.

Chapter 3 Manchester

The Education of Women at Manchester University 1883–1933, MUP 1941, by Mabel (Pythian) Tylecote BA Ph.D, formerly Assistant Lecturer in History at the University; *Owens College Magazine*. Ray Strachey's *The Cause* gives the general background and major personalities in the women's suffrage movement at the time that Esther joined it. The City of Manchester PRO has produced an excellent small book, *Men and Women of Manchester*, 1978, that lists all those great reformers and the reforming theories that came from this city. The most important book on the Northern suffrage movement is *One Hand Tied Behind Us* by Jill Liddington and Jill Norris, Virago, 1978. There is an unpublished thesis by S. M. Bryan, 'The Women's Suffrage Question in the Manchester Area 1890–1906', MA, Manchester 1977.

Chapter 4 Eva Gore-Booth becomes a suffragist

The early history of the University Settlement was extensively recorded in the *Owens College Magazine*; Teresa Billington Greig's papers held in the Fawcett Library give an account of early days in the Settlement; *Fifty Years in Every Street* by M. D. Stocks is a good source especially on the buildings of the Settlement.

There is an unpublished thesis on *Manchester and Salford Trades Council from 1880* by L. Bather, Ph.D, Manchester 1956.

It is most important to read Edward Carpenter's books from this period from cover to cover, and, without hindsight, to understand the effect of his writings upon women at the time that they were published. There is a growing tendency to play down Carpenter's influence or to deny the revolutionary nature of his ideas. Sheila Jeffrey's invaluable *The Spinster and Her Enemies. Feminism and Sexuality 1880–1930* does him something of an injustice in over-pruned quotations.

Chapter 5 Some suffragists become radical

Eva Gore-Booth and Esther Roper were so thoroughly embedded in the machinery of suffrage organisation that it is very rare to find them mentioned outside lists. Roger Fulford, *Votes for Women*, London 1957, and Andrew Rosen, *Rise Up Women, The Militant Campaign of the WSPU 1903–1914*, London 1974, both pay tribute to them.

Memoirs from Northern women in the suffrage campaign are necessary reading: Hannah Mitchell, *The Hard Way Up*, London 1977; Ada Nield Chew, *The Life and Writings of a Working Woman*, London 1982; and *The Life and Times of a Respectable Rebel, Selina Cooper 1864–1946*, Jill Liddington, London 1984, are indispensable.

Chapter 6 Eva Gore-Booth and Christabel Pankhurst

Christabel Pankhurst, *Unshackled*, London 1959; Emmeline Pankhurst, *My Own Story*, London 1914; Sylvia Pankhurst, *The Suffragette Movement*, London 1977; T. Billington Greig, *The Militant Suffrage Movement*, London 1911; Helena Swanwick, *I Have Been Young*, London 1935; Ramsay MacDonald, *Margaret Ethel MacDonald. A Memoir*, London 1912. *The Barmaid* is on microfilm at the Fawcett Library. In the Autumn of 1911 Esther Roper wrote a pamphlet for the Men's League for Women's Suffrage called 'The Case for the Pit Brow Worker'.

Chapter 7 Division in the suffrage movement

Unpublished thesis by C. E. Leech, 'The Feminist Movement in Manchester, 1903–1914', MA, Manchester 1971. Pamphlet by Eva Gore-Booth, *Women Workers and Parliamentary Representation*, published by L&CWT&OWRC, c. 1904; also by Eva Gore-Booth, 'Woman and the Suffrage: A Reply', in *Living Age*, 259 (1908), 140, and *Women's Right to Work*, Manchester & Salford Women's Trade and Labour Council, c. 1908.

Eva Gore-Booth's best-known published contribution to the suffrage cause comes from this period in *The Case for Women's Suffrage*, T. Fisher Unwin, 1907. The cover is plate no. 00; she was co-author with a remarkable group of names.

There was an enormous diversity of opinion amongst women on the suffrage question. Brian Harrison's *Separate Spheres: The Opposition to Women's Suffrage in Britain*, London 1978, identifies a type of woman that should not be forgotten, and Andro Linklater in *An Unhusbanded Life: Charlotte Despard, Suffragette, Socialist and Sinn*

Feiner, London 1980, describes the life of a woman who came to work with the Pankhursts and then took a different path.

Chapter 8 The Irish rebellion

Michael Begnal, 'Eva Gore-Booth on Behalf of Roger Casement, an unpublished appeal', Eire-Ireland, 6, no. 1 (1971), 11–16. Eva Gore-Booth's poems inspired by the 1916 rebellion were published in Dublin, 1917, in the volume *Broken Glory*.

Chapter 9 Last writings: the Gospel of Love and *Urania*

Urania, incomplete run, can be read at the Fawcett Library. *The Woman's Bible* was first published in 1895–8 but there is now a paperback available, Edinburgh 1985, with an introduction by Dale Spender. Madame Blavatsky wrote a vast work on Theosophy, *The Secret Doctrine: The Synthesis of Science, Religion and Philosophy*, 2nd edn, London 1888.

Chapter 10 World War One: peace and retirement

There is an article by Jill Liddington in *Over Our Dead Bodies. Women against the Bomb* called 'The Women's Peace Crusade: The History of a Forgotten Campaign' that gives details of one of Eva and Esther's interests at this time, though only Eva makes it into the lists. *Pioneers for Peace: The Women's International League for Peace and Freedom 1915–1965* by Gertrude Bussey and Margaret Tims, London 1965, similarly only mentions them in lists of signatures.

Eva Gore-Booth spoke at a conference on the Pacifist Philosophy of Life on 8 June 1915 printed later as *Religious Aspects of Non-Resistance*, Peace and Freedom Pamphlets, no. 3, London, League for Peace & Freedom, 1915.

Arthur Marwick *Women at War*, London 1977, gives an exciting illustrated account of the work done by women in the First World War.

Esther as well as Eva returned to the studies of her youth in her retirement. She produced a text-book for an SPCK series: *Select Passages illustrating Florentine Life in the Thirteenth and Fourteenth Centuries* (Texts for Students, no. 19, 1920). Her introduction explains the interest of the period to her: 'in the 13th and 14th centuries the practice of government based on Trade Guilds was in the process of development.'

BIBLIOGRAPHY

Works by Eva Gore-Booth

Poems, Longmans, London, 1898.

New Songs, A Lyric Selection made by AE from poems by Eva Gore-Booth and others, Dublin, 1904.

The One and the Many, Longmans, London, 1904.

Unseen Kings, Longmans, London, 1904.

The Three Resurrections and the Triumph of Maeve, Longmans, London, 1905.

The Egyptian Pillar, Maunsel, Dublin, 1907.

The Sorrowful Princess, Longmans, London, 1907.

The Agate Lamp, Longmans, London, 1912.

The Perilous Light, Erskine MacDonald, London, 1915.

Broken Glory, Maunsel, Dublin, 1917.

The Sword of Justice, London, 1918.

A Psychological and Poetic Approach to the Study of Christ in the Fourth Gospel, Longmans, London, 1923.

The Shepherd of Eternity, Longmans, London, 1925.

The House of Three Windows, Longmans, London, 1926.

The Inner Kingdom, Longmans, London, 1926.

The World's Pilgrim, Longmans, London, 1927.

Collected Poems of Eva Gore-Booth, with 'The Inner Life of a Child', Letters and a Biographical Introduction, Longmans, 1929.

The Buried Life of Deirdre, Longmans, London, 1930.

Other

Billington Greig, T. (1911), *The Militant Suffrage Movement*, Frank Palmer, London.

Blackburn, H. (1902), *Women's Suffrage*, Williams and Norgate, London.

Blavatsky, H. (1888), *The Secret Doctrine: The Synthesis of Science, Religion and Philosophy*, Theosophical Publishing, London.

Blunt, J. H. (1874), *Dictionary of Sects, Heresies, Ecclesiastical Parties and Schools of Religious Thought*, Rivingtons, London.

Cady Stanton, E. (1985), *The Woman's Bible. The Original Feminist Attack on the Bible*, Polygon Books, Edinburgh.

Carpenter, E. (1896), *Love's Coming of Age*, Allen and Unwin, London.

Carpenter, E. (ed.) (1897), *Forecasts of the Coming Century*, Labour Press, Manchester.

Carpenter, E. (1916), *My Days and Dreams*, Allen and Unwin, London.

Cullen Owen, R. (1984), *Smashing Times: A History of the Irish Women's Suffrage Movement*, Attic Press, Dublin.

Davies, M. Ll. (1904), *The Women's Co-Operative Guild 1883–1904*, W.C-O.G. Kirby Lonsdale, Westmor land.

Davies, M. Ll. (ed.) (1977), *Life as We Have Known It*, Virago, London.

Faderman, L. (1983), *Surpassing the Love of Men. Romantic Friendship and Love Between Women from the Renaissance to the Present*, Junction Books, London.

Fawcett, M. G. (1911), *Women's Suffrage*, T. & E. Jack, London.

Fawcett, M. G. (1920), *The Women's Victory and After. Personal Reminiscences 1911–1918*, Sidgwick and Jackson, London.

Fawcett, M.G. (1924), *What I Remember*, T. Fisher Unwin, London.

Fulford, R. (1958), *Votes for Women*, Faber and Faber, London.

Gaskell, E., paperback reprints 1987 in the OUP World's Classics series: *Mary Barton* (1848), *Ruth* (1853), *North and South* (1855).

Hamilton, C. (1909), *Marriage as a Trade*, Chapman and Hall, London.

Hamilton, C. (1935), *Life Errant*, Dent.

Jeffreys, S. (1985), *The Spinster and her Enemies. Feminism and Sexuality 1880–1930*, Pandora, London.

Jenkins, R. (1964), *Asquith*, Collins, London.

Liddington, J. (1984), *The Life and Times of a Respectable Rebel. Selina Cooper 1864–1946*, Virago, London.

Liddington, J. and Norris, J. (1978), *One Hand Tied Behind Us. The Rise of the Women's Suffrage Movement*, Virago, London.

Linklater, A. (1980), *An Unhusbanded Life. Charlotte Despard, Suffragette, Socialist and Sinn Feiner*, Hutchinson, London.

Lyons, F. S. L. (1975), *Ireland Since the Famine*, Fontana, London.

Kingsley, C. (1983), *Alton Locke*, OUP, Oxford.

MacDonald, J. R. (1912), *Margaret Ethel MacDonald. A Memoir*, Hodder & Stoughton, London.

Magnusson, M. (1978), *Landlord or Tenant? A View of Irish History*, Bodley Head, London.

Mairet, P. (1936), *A.R. Orage*, Dent, London.

Marreco, A. (1967), *The Rebel Countess*, Weidenfeld and Nicolson, London.

Marwick, A. (1977), *Women at War 1914–1918*, Fontana, London.

Mason, B. (1912), *The Story of the Women's Suffrage Movement*, Sheraton & Hughes, Manchester.

Middleton, L. (1977), *Women in the Labour Movement*, Croom Helm, London.

Pankhurst, C. (1959), *Unshackled*, Hutchinson, London.

Pankhurst, E. (1914), *My Own Story*, Eveleigh Nash, London.

Pankhurst, E. S. (1977), *The Suffragette Movement*, Virago, London.

Pethick-Lawrence, E. (1938), *My Part In A Changing World*, Gollancz, London.

Reid, B.L. (1976), *The Lives of Roger Casement*, Yale University Press.

Roper, E. (ed.) (1929), *Collected Poems of Eva Gore-Booth*, Longmans, London.

Roper, E. (ed.) (1934), *Prison Letters of Countess Markievicz*, Longmans, London.

Rosen, A. (1974), *Rise Up, Women!*, Routledge and Kegan Paul, London.

Rowbotham, S. (1973), *Hidden From History*, Pluto, London.

Rowbotham, S. (1973), *Woman's Consciousness: Man's World*, Penguin, London.

Schreiner, O. (1911), *Woman and Labour*, Fisher Unwin, London.

Stocks, M. (1945), *Fifty Years in Every Street*, Manchester University Press.

Stocks, M. (1949), *Eleanor Rathbone*, Gollancz, London.

Stocks, M. (1953), *The WEA. The First Fifty Years*, Allen and Unwin, London.

Stocks, M. (1970), *My Commonplace Book. An Autobiography*, Peter-Davies, London.

Strachey, R. (1931), *Millicent Garrett Fawcett*, John Murray, London.

Strachey, R. (1978), *The Cause. A Short History of the Women's Movement in Great Britain*, Virago, London.

Sullivan, A. M. (1952), *The last Serjeant. The Memoirs of Serjeant A.M. Sullivan, Q.C.*, Macdonald, London.

Swanwick, H. (1908), *Women in Industry from Seven Points of View*, Duckworth, London.

Swanwick, H. (1935), *I Have Been Young*, Gollancz, London.

Swanwick, H. (1938), *Roots of Peace*, Cape, London.

Taylor, B. (1983), *Eve and the New Jerusalem. Socialism and Feminism in the Nineteenth Century*, Virago, London.

Thompson, D. (ed.) (1983), *Over Our Dead Bodies. Women Against the Bomb*, Virago, London.

Tylecote, M. (1941), *The Education of Women at Manchester University 1883–1933*, Manchester University Press.

van Voris, J. (1967), *Constance de Markievicz. In the Cause of Ireland.* The University of Massachusets Press

Vicinus, M. (1973), *Suffer and Be Still: Women in the Victorian Age*, Bloomington.

Vicinus, M. (1977), *A Widening Sphere*, Bloomington.

Webb, C. (1927), *The Woman with the Basket*. Women's Co-operative Guild, Manchester.

Weeks, J. (1977), *Coming Out: Homosexual Politics in Britain from the Nineteenth Century to the Present*, Quartet, London.

White, J. and Wynne, M. (1963), *Irish Stained Glass*, Gill, Dublin.

Wiltsher, A. (1985), *Most Dangerous Women. Feminist Peace Campaigners of the Great War*, Pandora, London.

INDEX

Order Form

Discovering Women's History	Deirdre Beddoe	£4.95 ☐
Kitty O'Shea	Mary Rose Callaghan	£7.95 ☐
Gluck: A Biography of Hannah Gluckstein	Diana Souhami	£17.95 ☐
Rosa Luxemburg: A Life	Elżbieta Ettinger	£5.95 ☐
The Parnell Sisters	Mary FitzGerald	£7.95 ☐
Local Heroines: A Women's History Gazetteer to England, Scotland and Wales	Jane Legget	£8.95 ☐
Eva Gore-Booth and Esther Roper	Gifford Lewis	£7.95 ☐
Jane and May Morris	Jan Marsh	£4.95 ☐
Ellen and Edy	Joy Melville	£5.95 ☐
This Narrow Place: Sylvia Townsend Warner and Valentine Ackland	Wendy Mulford	£5.95 ☐
Charlotte Despard	Margaret Mulvihill	£7.95 ☐
Women of Letters	Phyllis Rose	£3.95 ☐
Constance Markiewicz	Anne Haverty	£7.95 ☐
Maud Gonne	Margaret Ward	£7.95 ☐
Suzanne Valadon	Felicity Edholm	£17.95 ☐

All these books are available at your local bookshop or newsagent or can be ordered direct by post. Just tick the titles you want and fill in the form below.

Name _____

Address _____

_____

_____

Send to: Unwin Hyman Cash Sales, PO Box 11, Falmouth, Cornwall TR10 9EN

Please enclose remittance to the value of the cover price plus:

UK: 60p for the first book plus 25p for the second book, thereafter 15p for each additional book ordered to a maximum charge of £1.90.

BFPO and EIRE: 60p for the first book plus 25p for the second book and 15p for the next 7 books and thereafter 9p per book.

OVERSEAS INCLUDING EIRE: £1.25 for the first book plus 75p for the second book and 28p for each additional book.

Unwin Paperbacks reserve the right to show new retail prices on covers which may differ from those previously advertised in the text or elsewhere. Postage rates are also subject to revision.